Before
EMINENT DOMAIN

STUDIES IN LEGAL HISTORY

*Published by the University of North Carolina Press
in association with the American Society for Legal History*

Daniel Ernst and Thomas A. Green, editors

Before EMINENT DOMAIN

Toward a History of Expropriation of Land for the Common Good

Susan Reynolds

THE UNIVERSITY OF
NORTH CAROLINA PRESS
Chapel Hill

© 2010 THE UNIVERSITY OF NORTH CAROLINA PRESS
All rights reserved

Designed and set in Arno Pro by Rebecca Evans
Manufactured in the United States of America

The paper in this book meets the guidelines for permanence
and durability of the Committee on Production Guidelines for
Book Longevity of the Council on Library Resources.

The University of North Carolina Press has been a
member of the Green Press Initiative since 2003.

Library of Congress Cataloging-in-Publication Data
Reynolds, Susan, 1929–
Before eminent domain: toward a history of expropriation
of land for the common good / Susan Reynolds.
p. cm. — (Studies in legal history)
Includes bibliographical references and index.
ISBN 978-0-8078-3353-7 (cloth: alk. paper)
ISBN 978-1-4696-2219-4 (pbk.: alk. paper)
1. Eminent domain — History. 2. Eminent domain —
History — To 1500. I. Title.
K3511.R49 2010
343'.0252 — dc22   2009033895
Earlier versions of parts of chapters 1–3 appeared as
"Compulsory Purchase in the Earlier Middle Ages," in
*Frankland: The Franks and the World of the Early Middle Ages;
Essays in Honor of Dame Jinty Nelson*, edited by Paul Fouracre and
David Ganz (Manchester: Manchester University Press, 2008).
Used by permission of the publisher.

cloth　14　13　12　11　10　　5　4　3　2　1
paper　18　17　16　15　14　　5　4　3　2　1

THIS BOOK WAS DIGITALLY PRINTED.

Contents

Acknowledgments vii

CHAPTER 1
Introduction
1.1 The Problem of Origins 1
1.2 Historians and Expropriation 7
1.3 The Evidence 9
1.4 The Plan and Scope of the Book 11

CHAPTER 2
Western Europe before 1100
2.1 Ancient Greece and Rome 15
2.2 The Problem of Evidence in the Early Middle Ages 16
2.3 Church Property 19
2.4 Fortifications 24
2.5 Other Probable Expropriations 27
2.6 Unjust Expropriations 29
2.7 Conclusion 31

CHAPTER 3

Western Europe and British North America, 1100–1800

3.1 The Plan of the Chapter 33
3.2 England 34
3.3 Italy 46
3.4 France 54
3.5 Germany 65
3.6 Spain 72
3.7 The English Colonies in America 77
3.8 Conclusion 83

CHAPTER 4

Justifications and Discussions

4.1 The Problem 85
4.2 Before Grotius 86
4.3 Grotius and After 94
4.4 Conclusion 108

CHAPTER 5

Communities, Individuals, and Property

5.1 The Problem 111
5.2.1 Before Grotius: Communities 112
5.2.2 Before Grotius: Individuals 123
5.2.3 Before Grotius: Property 127
5.3 Grotius and After 130
5.4 Conclusion 138

Works Cited 141
Index 169

Acknowledgments

Over the past few years I have made a number of friends and colleagues listen to my ramblings about expropriation for the public good. I am grateful to all of them for listening and discussing and especially to those who gave me references to cases or discussions I did not know of, namely: David Bates, Brenda Bolton, Paul Brand, David Carpenter, Edward Cooper, Pauline Croft, Wendy Davies, David Ganz, George Gretton, Jocelyn Hillgarth, Bridgett Jones, Derek Keene, Frédérique Lachaud, Vickie Macnair, and Romila Thapar. I am also grateful to Tim Macfarland and Klaske Muizelaar for translating bits of, respectively, medieval German and sixteenth-century Dutch, and to David Ganz for references on the use of *res publica* in the early Middle Ages.

In 2005 I used earlier versions of parts of the book in lectures to the American Society for Legal History and to a seminar at the University of Aberdeen. I am grateful for the comments of both audiences and in particular to David Dumville at Aberdeen for reading the lecture afterwards and, among other useful comments, for confirming my suspicion that he could find no reference to the acquisition of land for Anglo-Saxon fortifications. In 2007 I used parts of what became chapter 5 in papers given at the earlier medieval seminar at the Institute of Historical Research, London, and at a conference in honor of Wendy Davies held at University College, London. Earlier versions of parts of chapters 1–3 were published as "Compulsory Purchase in the Earlier

Middle Ages," in *Frankland: The Franks and the World of the Early Middle Ages; Essays in Honor of Dame Jinty Nelson*, edited by Paul Fouracre and David Ganz (Manchester, 2008). I am grateful to Manchester University Press for permission to use these again. As ever, I have found the British Library, the Institute of Historical Research, the Institute of Advanced Legal Studies, the University of London Senate House Library, and the Warburg Institute wonderful places to work. Librarians at them all have been very kind, but I must mention especially the friendly helpfulness and patience of those who fetch and carry books at the British Library. They are amazing.

I also owe thanks to Charles Donahue, Thomas A. Green, and an anonymous reader for the University of North Carolina Press. All three made extremely useful suggestions and corrections. John K. Wilson has been a meticulous copy editor. Above all I thank Tom Green for being such a wonderfully sympathetic, constructive, and sharp-eyed editor.

Before
EMINENT DOMAIN

CHAPTER 1

Introduction

1.1 THE PROBLEM OF ORIGINS

In October 1905 F. W. Maitland wrote a letter to the secretary of the Selden Society in which he remarked:

> I have often wondered where the Americans found their eminent domain — or rather how they came to borrow just this from the continental sources. Has it ever struck you that what protected us against this was the completeness of our feudalism? Unquestionably we all hold of the King, but the lord has no right to "expropriate" the tenant. Just because there is supreme landlordship there is no eminent domain in the foreign sense.[1]

Maitland died just over a year later, so that, what with his teaching, involvement with the Selden Society, writing the life of Leslie Stephen, and struggling with illness, it is not surprising that he never got around to exploring the history of eminent domain. In the century since he wrote those words, various people have engaged with bits of the subject, but no one seems to have attempted a general history of what can better be called "expropriation of land for the common good." I prefer not to call it "eminent domain" in the American fashion for three reasons: first, because the

---

1. Maitland, *Letters*, ed. Fifoot, no. 449. He referred to the eminent domain of the modern state in Pollock and Maitland, *History of English Law*, 2:3.

expression seems to have come into use in the United States only from the 1790s and to have been restricted to the United States;[2] second, because the American usage slightly distorts the meaning given to the term by Hugo Grotius (1583–1645), from whom it is derived; and third, because it can be taken to imply that land may be taken because the state holds a superior layer of property right. That, I shall argue, never seems to have been its justification. The common British use of "compulsory purchase" is even more odd, since what is compulsory is surely the sale, not the purchase. I have therefore decided to follow the civil law tradition, which uses the word "expropriation" or its equivalent (e.g., *espropriazione, expropiación, Enteignung*), unless I need to draw attention to a word in the source I cite. This essay does not attempt a complete history of expropriation for the common, or public, good. All it does is attempt to open up the subject and suggest lines of future research. It starts with the earliest evidence I have found but ends in 1800, after which there is much more material that has already been written about extensively by lawyers and legal historians.

Much legal history has been written to follow up Maitland's discoveries and suggestions about medieval law. Some of it has shown that he made mistakes, but none of the mistakes have shaken my belief that the combination of historical imagination with deep and exact learning makes him the greatest of legal historians and one of the greatest historians of the Middle Ages. I remain convinced of that even though, having been drawn into the subject of expropriation by the remark I quoted, I have to start by saying that his suggestion about its absence from England was inexplicable — even nonsensical. Whatever he meant by "eminent domain in the foreign sense," it is difficult to see any real difference between that and what, even if he had not thought about earlier expropriations ostensibly made for the public good, he must have known as the taking of land for railways. I shall also argue that feudalism, whether in England or elsewhere, seems to have had

2. See chapters 3.7 at nn. 182–83 and 4.3 at nn. 78–80.

very little to do with it at any date. Such evidence as I have found does not support either the belief of the American judge who in 1935 saw the right of eminent domain as a relic of feudalism[3] or Maitland's guess that feudalism might have protected the English against expropriation by governmental authority. I am comforted by the fact that his remarks were merely thrown out casually in a letter to a friend and also by my suspicion that he would have been more interested in new information and hypotheses than in having his casual guess confirmed or rejected.

So far as historians have been interested in expropriation for what is claimed to be the common good, they have generally concentrated on its modern history, since the building of railways, roads, and airports and the demolition of slums or planning of towns have made it both common and contested. Its history before 1800 is problematical. Those who have studied it have tended either to start with Grotius and later writers on natural law or to go back to the recovery of Roman law and the rise of communal activity in twelfth-century Europe.[4] I suggest that the history of expropriation for the common good is longer, more complicated, and much wider than either of these explanatory outlines implies.

My hypothesis is that in any settled society in which individuals or groups have acknowledged rights in particular pieces of land there may be some occasions, like the digging of drainage or irrigation channels, or the building of roads or fortifications, on which such rights may come into conflict with the needs of the community as a whole, however it is defined and ruled. Different societies may have different ways of reconciling the rights of individuals with the needs of the group, according to their different economies and legal systems; some societies may have several different ways of doing so, according to the nature of the conflicting interests; and some may have no accepted way of taking land from

---

3. Stoebuck, "General Theory," 557.
4. Lenhoff, "Development of the Concept," 596.

individuals for collective use. I do not claim that expropriation for the common good is found in every society where individuals have rights in land, but only that I have found enough evidence of it in enough societies to make looking for it worthwhile.

For land to be taken from individuals, but only for the supposed good of the community and in return for some kind of compensation, implies that the individuals whose land is taken have rights in it that are recognized by their society. Historians have sometimes denied that particular past societies allowed individuals to have rights in land that amounted to what the historians considered real or true rights of property. Some have maintained that under régimes that seemed strange to them, such as those they called "Oriental Despotism" and "Feudalism," all the land belonged to the rulers, whether emperors, kings, or chiefs, so that none of their subjects had defensible rights in the land they occupied. These simplistic views of societies and rights that looked strange to outsiders have not been confirmed when measured against the various rights and obligations actually attached to land in practice in any particular society. According to the anthropologist Lucy Mair, Europeans who arrived in some African societies found nobody who could say, or was interpreted to mean, "I own this land, and if you want to buy it I am the man to apply to." The Europeans, she says, might then conclude that "Primitive land rights are communal." If, on the other hand, they were told that the chief owned the land and maybe that he owned everything in it, they concluded that no one else had any rights in it against him.[5] As she and others have shown, neither conclusion was justified. Rights in land are never absolute, but their limitations differ in different societies. They are limited in our own, even if they are dignified by words like "true property rights," or "ownership," as "understood in a mature legal system."[6] In order to judge whether land is held by what can be considered real or true rights

---

5. Mair, *Introduction to Social Anthropology*, 138.
6. Honoré, "Ownership."

of property that are worth comparing with those with which we are familiar, we need to look at them more closely. They need to be analyzed by separating the bundles of rights that are taken for granted in different societies, including our own, into specific rights and obligations that seem to be attached to land and maybe to different classes of landholding.[7] In considering expropriation for the common good, the first point to consider is whether individuals in the society one is looking at have rights in land that are judged to be valid in that society. If so, one question to be tackled is whether any particular bundle of rights, or any particular piece of land, although considered to deserve protection in the society concerned, was nevertheless vulnerable to expropriation. The next question is whether the expropriated landholder was supposed to be compensated. The rules about expropriation I have found or, more often, deduced from practice in the parts of western Europe where I have looked for it do not seem to have varied according to the varying status of land or landholder. This makes the question whether any bundle of rights matches the particular bundle that is called ownership, or true property, in our society even less relevant than it is in a more general study of property rights.[8]

Some modern writers see the right to exclude others as an important characteristic of property,[9] but this has not been the case in all societies, even those with well-established rules and rights in land. In the European Middle Ages and in colonial America, people with what their societies considered full rights might have to submit to common rights over their land at certain times of the year. Sometimes they had to allow the taking of materials from

---

7. Reynolds, *Fiefs and Vassals*, 53–57, and "Did All the Land Belong to the King?"

8. On bundles of rights and "ownership": Allott, "Family Property"; Bennett, "Terminology"; Donahue, "Future of the Concept"; Penner, "'Bundle of Rights'"; Gordon, "Paradoxical Property"; James W. Harris, "Reason or Mumbo Jumbo."

9. E.g., Merrill, "Property and the Right to Exclude."

their land, without compensation, for building roads, fortifications, or other purposes considered to be in the public interest.[10] A landowner's rights have sometimes also been combined with other individuals' right to take certain sorts of produce or even to cultivate land that the owner was not using.[11] Individuals with recognized rights, whether permanent or temporary, are still often subject to various kinds of incursions in the public interest, like control of watercourses or wayleave (i.e., an easement or, in civil law terms, a servitude) for electricity lines. In all societies the fullest rights in land known to the society are restricted in one way or another. In the past, owners' rights to hunt or mine in what was recognized as their own property were sometimes restricted, while nowadays planning or zoning controls are often imposed on otherwise full property. Obvious examples of ways in which the rights of property have often been subjected to public needs are the taking of taxes, dues, and services from landowners.

I shall not discuss any of these partial subordinations of individual property to common needs, though including them would mean taking a much more realistic view of the frequently fragmented character of property rights than may be implied by ignoring them. It would, however, make the subject too large and complex for a preliminary foray like this. I am also going to exclude such rights of rulers or other lords, like the right to taxes, as did not deprive landowners of the title to their land. In medieval Europe these might, for instance, include the right to take supplies from land for their courts or armies (*fodrum*, purveyance or *prises*); to have lodging for themselves, their courts, or their

---

10. The boundary between taking materials and taking the land itself could be hard to draw: see, e.g., "Querimoniae Normannorum," no. 73; petition about a quarry in the Forest of Dean (Gloucestershire), Ancient Petitions, SC 8/326, no. E 731, National Archives, London (transcript given me by Dr Paul Brand).

11. E.g. Firth, *Primitive Polynesian Economy*, 259–64, and other works cited in nn. 24–25 below.

armies (*albergum, gistum, hospitalitas, hospitatio, mansionaticum*); or to take over fortresses in time of need (rendition, rendability). Nor am I going to consider the confiscation of land as a penalty or to pay the owner's debts, or its taking for redistribution in order to secure greater equality (nationalization). This last is easy to leave out since it has happened mostly after my closing date of 1800. I am concerned only with the taking of individual pieces of land, extinguishing all title, rights, or claim the owner or tenant might have, and doing so, not for social justice, nor as a punishment for crime, nor to pay the owner's debts, but because this piece of land was needed (or was said to be needed) for public use or the common good. My argument will be that in all the periods and in all the societies that I have considered, the right of the community to take land for the common good, with compensation to the owner, seems to have been taken for granted. There is no period in which I have found evidence that it was seen as an innovation.

From now on I shall, for brevity, refer simply to "expropriation" when I mean the taking of land for the common or public good. If I need to mention the taking of land either from individuals as a penalty or to pay debts, or from whole classes of owners for redistribution to others, I shall use the word "confiscation."

1.2 HISTORIANS AND EXPROPRIATION

Considering the one sort of expropriation I have chosen is difficult enough. First, because, although there may be much that I have not read, secondary works on the subject seem to be surprisingly rare. Historians of politics have a lot to say about taxation and sometimes about penal confiscation or other burdens on property, but little about the possibility of expropriation and its political implications. That may be because it generally affected individuals and often only small pieces of land, so that it did not ignite political controversies at the time. Nevertheless, the acceptance of a rule of expropriation, even with compensation, implies that the needs of a community are assumed to override the rights of its members to their property.[12] It is therefore surprising that historians of political thought concerned with periods in which arguments about property rights or the relation of individuals to society loomed large have not said more about expropriation. Such works as I have found that expressly deal with expropriation, and that I mention in later chapters, on the other hand, do not generally seem to be concerned with the implications of the practice for ideas about society and politics.

Those who analyze property rights in general similarly seem to devote little attention to the ways that apparently secure rights may be lost without any fault of the owner — just as most of them seem to be less interested in the obligations, as opposed to the rights, of property or in societies outside modern Europe and America.[13] As for lawyers and legal historians, Americans seem to have done more than the British on what they call "takings"[14] of property in England, but they concentrate — reasonably enough — mostly on American law and the problems of compensation.[15] On the Middle Ages, Antonio Pertile produced a notable list of Italian expropriations and Hans Planitz a few for German towns.[16] I have found material about the ideas of academic lawyers since the twelfth century from writers in the civil law tradition, especially

---

12. This is discussed in chapter 5.

13. E.g., Honoré, "Ownership"; Ryan, *Property*; Waldron, *Right to Private Property*; Anderson and McChesney, *Property Rights*. Expropriation is mentioned briefly by Becker, *Property Rights*, 29–30, 129 n. 13; by Reeve, *Property*, 21–22, 40–41; and by Ellickson, "Property in Land," 1384. Paul, *Property Rights*, has one essay, and Munzer, *Theory of Property*, two chapters, that discuss expropriation but only in the American context.

14. Was the word first taken perhaps from Blackstone, *Commentaries*, 3:145 (III.9), though there it is applied to movables?

15. E.g., Sackman, *Nichols' The Law*, 1:68–78; Lewis, *Treatise on the Law*; Lenhoff, "Development of the Concept"; Stoebuck, "General Theory"; Paul, *Property Rights*, 71–184.

16. Pertile, *Storia*, 4:354–62; Planitz, *Die deutsche Stadt*, 321–22.

Ugo Nicolini, and some in more general works on such subjects as urban history or the history of roads.[17] A good deal of what I have found concentrates on the evidence of legislation rather than practice, sometimes assuming that the legislation was more innovatory than the evidence of practice suggests it was. Some of the essays on expropriation in different countries or other aspects of the subject in two recent volumes of the Recueils de la Société Jean Bodin have been particularly useful.[18] All these and some others are cited, some with comments, in the sections of chapter 3 dealing with the relevant countries, while works that touch on academic discussions are referred to in chapter 4.

1.3 THE EVIDENCE

My second and more serious difficulty concerns the evidence itself. Even when there is enough evidence to suggest that expropriation in the public interest was in principle allowed, references to it are often hard to find. I suspect that in many societies pressure from public opinion and the acceptance of social norms ensured that only the most awkward or powerful characters objected to surrendering their property to common needs. That may mean that many expropriations went unrecorded, at least in writings that have survived. Even where there is a record, the justification was often not stated but merely implied, which suggests that the justice of expropriation for the common or public good was taken for granted. Where the common or public good is mentioned, I have often cited the actual words used. Where it is implied, I have tried to explain from the context why I deduce it. I have not, in-

---

17. Ugo Nicolini, *La proprietà*; Domat, *Les loix civiles*, 1:51–52 (pt. 1, I. tit. 2, §13); Dareste and Dareste, *La justice administrative*, 121–23, 453–61, 587–89; Erler and Kaufmann, *Handwörterbuch zur deutschen Rechtsgeschichte*, vol. 1, cols. 941–44.

18. *L'expropriation*, RSJB 66 (1999) and 67 (2000).

cidentally, found any distinction between public good and public use being discussed or worried about before my closing date of 1800.[19]

In such records as I have found in the printed sources on which this essay is almost entirely based, the difference between a voluntary and compulsory sale of land by an individual to the ruler or rulers of a community on its behalf is sometimes invisible or hard to detect. One example of this uncertainty is a story in the second book of Samuel, which in its present form is said to date from the sixth century B.C.E.[20] When a plague was ravaging Israel, the prophet Gad told King David to build an altar on the threshing floor of Araunah the Jebusite. When David told Araunah he wanted to buy his threshing floor for an altar, Araunah offered it as a gift, but David insisted on paying for it because it would be wrong to give God something that cost the giver nothing. The plague stopped.[21] While this was not quite compulsory expropriation, let alone evidence of an established practice, it suggests attitudes that would fit the norms that lie behind the practice: the obligation to give up something for the common good but the right to be compensated for it. In another biblical story, King Ahab's seizure of Naboth's vineyard does not qualify: though governments through history have often succeeded in passing off their interest as that of the common or public good, Ahab failed to do so. That was perhaps partly because, when Naboth refused to sell, Queen Jezebel had him falsely accused and executed, but also because the story suggests that Ahab's wish to turn the vineyard into a herb garden looked like pure selfishness.[22]

I am prepared to argue that there were far more expropriations

---

19. On the distinction, see chapter 4 at nn. 76–77.
20. Barton and Muddiman, *Oxford Bible Commentary*, 197–200, 230.
21. 2 Samuel (2 Kings, in the Vulgate Bible) 24:15–25, King James Version (KJV).
22. 1 Kings (3 Kings, in the Vulgate Bible) 21, KJV. See also the predictions of seizures by kings in 1 Samuel 8:6, 11, 14.

in less well recorded societies than the few references I have found suggest. That is not merely because there is so much more to be found, but because some of the references I have found imply, for instance, that the taking of land without compensation was assumed at the time to be wrong. My argument is that the principle that land might be taken from individuals when the community needed it has been so generally accepted that it did not need to be stated or argued about until quite recent times. The apparent lack of legislation about it is, paradoxically, a strong argument for this. I have found examples of legislation regulating the compensation to be made in particular circumstances or types of expropriation, but none earlier than the eighteenth-century codifications and constitutions that dealt with the actual right of governments or communities to expropriate. Even then, they regulated the right rather than established it, in effect stating what, given the evidence of practice, was already accepted in law: that is, that land could be taken only for the common good and with compensation.[23] The Bill of Rights added to the American Constitution, for instance, was concerned only with compensation, apparently assuming the liability of land to expropriation for the public good. As for the need for compensation, that, far from being the result of progress or popular government, seems to have been long accepted in many societies. The problem was and is the difficulty of assessing the just amount to be paid in any particular case and, in cases when those to be compensated have no power or influence, of getting it actually paid.

1.4 THE PLAN AND SCOPE OF THE BOOK

Chapters 2 and 3 survey the evidence I have found of the actual practice of expropriation, which has convinced me that it is impossible to accept arguments that it started either in the twelfth century, as a result of new communal movements or new legal

---

23. See chapter 3 at nn. 112, 139, 141, 184, and chapter 4 at nn. 50, 75.

learning, or still later with the emergence of sovereign governments and new ideas about natural law. The evidence about the areas of western Europe before 1100 C.E. that I discuss in chapter 2 is extremely slight, though others may well find more. After 1100 there is much more, so that in chapter 3 I can survey separately what I have found for several different countries in western Europe, ending with that from the British colonies in America. Again, however, there may well be more evidence than I have found since my knowledge of the background of societies, economies, and law after the Middle Ages is sparse. The sections on postmedieval Italy, Germany, and Spain contain, I hope, just enough information to suggest that land probably went on being taken with compensation, at least on occasion and in some areas, until my stopping point in 1800.

Chapter 4 surveys such justifications and arguments about the principle of expropriation as I have found in the European and North American texts between the twelfth and eighteenth centuries. Just because the principle was, as I argue, so taken for granted, the justifications are rather disappointing: the only really serious arguments I have found that went to the fundamental issue of the relation between communities and the property rights of their members were made by Hugo Grotius and some of his immediate followers.

Finally, in chapter 5, I discuss the ideas about politics and society that might explain why the obligation to surrender property for what was considered the general good has been so widely accepted. This is relatively easy to understand before the seventeenth century when, as I argue, ideas about secular government started from the premise of the existence of peoples that formed natural, given communities. The general good of each community was therefore assumed to be the chief purpose of government. What I have found harder to explain is the way that the obligation to surrender property to the common good survived with so little argument into more modern times when individual rights were often given priority.

I should like to have considered expropriation in areas outside western Europe and British North America, but even the areas I have dealt with proved to be more than I could thoroughly investigate. I can hardly do more than speculate about the rest of the world. With respect to Africa, I found a few references from social anthropologists: one possible case in central Nigeria and three in southern Africa. All of them more or less clearly, though in different ways, imply that land could be taken if it was needed for the public good or with general consent and required compensation by allocation of other land.[24] There may well be other cases that I have not found in the anthropologists' reports I have read, though I suspect that some anthropologists have been more interested in other aspects of property customs, like inheritance, than in expropriation. Some traditional African societies did not use land in such a way as to produce the kind of rights that might give rise to expropriation, or found other ways to reconcile collective and individual rights, as did the Tikopia of Polynesia.[25]

The great and complex societies of the Middle East, India, and China should produce more evidence one way or another, but my very sketchy and elementary reading suggests that legal historians of these areas have tended to concentrate more on treatises, principles, and legislation than on the kind of evidence of practice that would be expected to produce references to expropriation. I suggest that members of local communities may have reckoned that they had rights in their holdings against their neighbors that were negotiated and disputed within the community. In such cases those communities may on occasion have taken

---

24. Bohannan and Bohannan, *Tiv Economy*, 82–88; Sheddick, *Land Tenure in Basutoland*, 129; Schapera, *Native Land Tenure*, 42, 181–82; Gluckman, *Ideas in Barotse Jurisprudence*, 80, 83, 141–45; Chinhengo, "Expropriation in Zimbabwe," 356–58. The dialogue reported in Gluckman, *Judicial Process among the Barotse*, 142–45, does not, however, refer to compensation.

25. Firth, *Primitive Polynesian Economy*, 17–18, 28, 59, 218–19, 259–64; cf. Allan, *Customary Land Tenure*, 116, 119–22.

land from individuals, as some seem to have done in Europe and Africa, without reference to a distant ruler.[26] Even though much of this may have been unrecorded, more evidence might be found if historians looked for it. It is tempting to wonder if some have been deterred from doing so by the survival of belief in so-called Oriental Despotism, under which all land belonged to the ruler.[27] Thanks to suggestions from Professor Romila Thapar, however, I have happened on two possible references for India. A Kashmiri king of the late ninth century C.E. gave compensation for lands he took from temples, and a local council in south India in the tenth century resolved to buy land to widen and repair a road.[28] I also have one chance reference to Turkey; an eighteenth-century Western traveler, the Baron de Tott, told how the sultan, after taking advice, made a compromise with a Jew who did not want to sell land to him for a mosque.[29] Beyond these stray examples, I leave the subject of expropriation in Asian societies to historians of Asia.

In the areas on which I have tried to find material, my searches have been entirely restricted to printed material, except for a very few manuscript sources available to me in London. What I have consulted is what I found by following up footnotes in such secondary works as included anything about expropriation, together with references given to me by friends whose ears I bent about the subject. Given all these limitations to my research, I am well aware that there is much more to be discovered about expropriation for the common good, whether in Europe, America, or anywhere else. But as I said before, this book is intended to do no more than open up the subject in the hope that others may explore it further.

26. Menski, *Indian Legal Systems*, 25–6, 33, and *Hindu Law*, 73, 122.
27. Ghoshal, *Agrarian System in Ancient India*, 95–102.
28. Kosambi, "Origins of Feudalism in Kashmir," 141; Nilakanta Sastri, *Studies*, 122.
29. Tott, *Mémoires*, 1:149–53. I am not sure if the lease was from the Sultan to the Jew or vice versa.

CHAPTER 2

Western Europe before 1100

2.1 ANCIENT GREECE AND ROME

Greece is certainly not part of western Europe, and only half, at most, of the Roman empire was, but it seems reasonable to say something about them here, if only because they are traditionally seen as the background to later European history. The Roman material is clearly relevant: although medieval lawyers do not seem to have used the texts in the Theodosian code or *Novellae* that dealt with actual expropriations, they used some from the *Codex* and *Digest* to argue about the emperor's jurisdiction and rights over his subjects' lands.

The evidence of possible expropriation in ancient Greece includes legislation for the valuation of noncitizens' property that might be wanted to build temples; the help, with provision for agreeing to valuations, that the new regime gave to those who chose to emigrate to Eleusis after a revolution in Athens, so that they could get consent of the owners of the houses they wanted; and perhaps the laying of drains in private fields in Euboea, with payment to the landowner.[1] About the position in the law of ancient Rome there can be no doubt, despite the traditional belief

1. Karabélias, "L'expropriation en droit grec ancien."

in the "absolute property" of Roman law.[2] The suggestion that expropriation was accepted by the time that public works in Rome begin to be recorded in the second century B.C.E. seems plausible. Apart from the obvious likelihood that the construction of Roman roads, fortifications, and public buildings would have needed some kind of expropriation, there are later references to actual cases when it took place and to the need for compensation.[3] In 412 C.E. the prefect of the city of Rome was told that the portico added to the Baths of Honorius was so fine that the slight neglect of private interests that it entailed would be just. The neglect was slight because anyone whose property was sacrificed was to receive public property in exchange.[4] According to Justinian, land could be taken even from churches for the public good (*ad reipublicae utilitatem*), provided that equal or greater property was given in exchange.[5] But, though emperors might authorize particular expropriations or deal with problems referred to them about compensation, it is not clear that only they could authorize the taking of property anywhere in the empire: local officials or the communities over which they presided seem, I deduce, to have had the right to do it for themselves, simply referring difficult cases about compensation to the emperor.

2.2 THE PROBLEM OF EVIDENCE IN THE EARLY MIDDLE AGES

The European Middle Ages are particularly important in the history of expropriation because it is from then that legal historians

---

2. E.g., Harouel, *Histoire*, 4–5; but cf. Schulz, *Classical Roman Law*, 338–39, and *Principles of Roman Law*, 29–31; Birks, "Roman Law Concept."
3. Matthews, "Valuation of Property"; Jones, "Expropriation in Roman Law"; Lozano Corbi, "¿Existió en la epoca republicana romana?"; Pennitz, "Die Enteignungsproblematik in Römischen Recht."
4. Mommsen and Meyer, *Codex Theodosianus*, 1:813–14 (15.1.50, 53).
5. Mommsen et al., *Corpus Iuris Civilis*, 3:53 (*Novellae* 7.2.1).

have sometimes traced the origin of the modern law, focusing especially on the recovery of Roman law and the rise of communal activity in the twelfth century.[6] Recently it has been suggested that expropriation began, at least in France, as an exercise of feudal seignorial power, in the lord's own interest, and was then tamed by the surrender of seignorial rights to towns and other collective groups.[7] The trouble with both these arguments is that they rely heavily, not only on the scarcity of evidence from before 1100, but on the assumption that communal solidarity and activity hardly existed until the twelfth century. I have argued elsewhere, as have others, that although evidence is scarce for the early Middle Ages, there is enough to suggest a good deal of collective activity, both local and at the level of kingdoms, and that this reflected assumptions and ideas about peoples and kingdoms as communities of descent, law, and political solidarity.[8] I shall say more in chapter 5 about the political ideas and assumptions that were involved.

The early medieval law codes do not seem to say anything about expropriation. One reason for that may be that there was relatively little need for direct, total expropriation, as opposed, for instance, to the collective regulation of arable land and pasture, which is clearly attested. Another reason may be that the general principles of giving up land for collective needs in return for compensation were taken for granted and that when it happened the land was given up to the local community without fuss or record. After all, as I shall argue in chapter 3, even when record keeping improved, there was for centuries very little in the way of direct

---

6. See, e.g., Meyer, *Das Recht der Expropriation*, 70–76; Ugo Nicolini, *La proprietà*, 93–97, and *Le limitazioni*, 20–21; Waelkens, "L'expropriation," and other authors in *L'expropriation*.

7. Mestre, "Les origines seigneuriales"; Gislain, "L'expropriation"; Harouel, "L'expropriation."

8. Reynolds, *Kingdoms and Communities*; and, e.g., Goetz, "Regnum"; Janet Nelson, "Kingship and Empire"; Fouracre, "Cultural Conformity"; Davies and Fouracre, *Settlement of Disputes*.

legislation to allow expropriation. I can nevertheless produce a few examples from other sources of what looks like the taking of property for the common good, in some cases at least in return for compensation, supplemented by other hints that something of the sort may have been happening. Slight and patchy as the evidence is, I propose nevertheless to argue that this may be due as much to the failure of historians to look for it because they think it is not there as it is to the poverty of the evidence. The increase in the evidence from the twelfth century need not reflect entirely new ideas about the common good. Rather, it may reflect the increase in record keeping in general, as well as a greater need of expropriation because of economic development and especially the growth of towns and fortifications.

If the law of expropriation had been derived, along with ideas about the common good, from Roman law, one might expect to find evidence from expropriations carried out in the Italian cities that embraced the new law so enthusiastically in the twelfth and early thirteenth centuries. There is indeed clear evidence for the taking of property for public use from twelfth-century Italy, but, as I shall argue, it does not give clear signs of influence from the Roman texts. Even before the first of my Italian examples, moreover, I have some from England, which were surely not reflections of Roman ideas.

So far as the seignorial origins of expropriation in France are concerned, I shall argue in chapter 3 that the evidence cited seems to come from too late to be convincing. One item of evidence from Spain, however, suggests that there kings may have claimed to take land at will. It is a charter issued by Alfonso VI of León and Castile in 1093 to the monastery of Sahagún. The preamble of the charter opens with the statement that it is lawful for kings and great men (*potentioribus hominibus*) to take land from individuals and give it to anyone they choose. The king goes on to say that he is giving to the monastery the land next to it on which his wife had built palaces (*palacios*) and other buildings. Whether the implication is that the property had been taken from Sahagún in the first place or had been taken from others is unclear.[9] It seems rash to assume, without corroborative evidence, that the opening statement of this charter was generally taken to be true, either in Spain or elsewhere. Whether it was or not, we should probably not assume without argument that what appear as royal or seignorial powers were normally exercised for purely selfish interests or that it was generally thought to be right that they should be. Kings and lesser lords may sometimes or often have taken land for more or less selfish reasons, like building castles or palaces for themselves, but all rulers, whether kings or lesser lords, were, as I argue further in chapter 5, supposed to act on behalf of the communities they ruled. Besides, though building palaces or castles may look selfish to modern eyes, the better evidence from after 1100 suggests that the palaces of rulers, like modern government buildings, were assumed to serve a public purpose, while castles and other fortifications passed the test even more obviously. In a period of sparse records like the early Middle Ages, it may therefore be rash to assume that an expropriation apparently done by a king or lord was not thought at the time to be done on behalf of the community he ruled and maybe after consultation with men who spoke on its behalf.

2.3 CHURCH PROPERTY

The most striking example in the early Middle Ages of what looks like a modified form of expropriation for the public good is what has traditionally been seen as the plundering, spoliation, or secularization of church land by Charles Martel and his descendants, the Carolingian kings and emperors.[10] Although they,

---

9. Mínguez Fernández, *Colección diplomatica de Sahagún*, vol. 3, no. 914.
10. Fouracre, *Age of Charles Martel*, 2–3, 121–26, 137–40, discusses both the evidence and the origin of the traditional interpretation.

like other rulers and lords, sometimes bullied the clergy, ejected bishops and gave their sees to others, and may have taken land from churches for their own selfish purposes, their most famous "spoliations" were made for what they claimed were the needs of defense. That Charles Martel used the church property he took to support his soldiers is suggested by what his son Carloman told a church council less than two years after Charles died. According to Bishop Boniface, Carloman at first promised to summon a council for his part of the kingdom in order to reform the church, which, according to Boniface, had long been crushed and despoiled. In the event Carloman told the council that, because of the threat of war from neighboring peoples, he had decided, with the advice of the clergy and Christian people, to keep the church property he already held for a while longer to support his army. Twelve pence would meanwhile be paid every year from each *casata* to the church to which the land belonged. If the holder of the land died, his holding would go back to the church, unless the prince (Carloman) was compelled by necessity to keep it, in which case he would make a new grant that would still preserve the church's ultimate rights. Churches in real poverty would be exempt.[11]

Much the same system of grants of church land by royal command, though with smaller rents to the churches, was continued by Charlemagne and extended to the Kingdom of Lombardy as well, apparently, as to his other conquests.[12] Not all of the property that found its way into the hands of the followers of kings or mayors of the palace probably got there because of urgent military needs. Such grants as were made to conciliate rivals or keep powerful subjects happy could nevertheless have been seen at the time as justified by the need to keep the peace within the kingdom: the boundary between the interests of a government and the welfare of the community of its subjects is never easy to draw. But while

---

11. *Epistolae Bonifatii et Lullii*, no. 50, p. 82; *Concilia Aevi Karolini*, no. 2, c. 2.

12. *Capitularia Regum Francorum*, vol. 1, no. 20, c. 9.

some grants of church land to laymen look as if they would not have been justifiable by the needs of the kingdom, others were justified, more or less explicitly, at the time and in that way.

According to the formal declarations of kings and councils, these Carolingian takings of church land ought not to count as full expropriation (or secularization), since churches were supposed to retain their ultimate title. This may partly explain why compensation was made — or was supposed to be made — by annual rents rather than lump sums. In practice, though kings periodically made promises to restore what had been taken and some holdings were indeed given back, restoration became politically and legally more difficult when land was left in the hands of families through generations or passed to people who knew nothing — or could claim to know nothing — of the church's title.[13] That happened partly because what started as an emergency turned out, as tends to happen with powers that governments take in emergencies, to last a long time. It also happened partly because some churches failed, for whatever reason, to collect rents and keep their records up to date. The most compelling reason of all, however, may have been the sheer inertia of customary law in the face of landholders in possession. As a result, much of the land that had been taken from churches to support eighth-century armies was still being held in much the same way in the eleventh century.[14]

Many bishops, abbots, and chroniclers no doubt resented what was taken from their own churches, and in the ninth century Archbishop Hincmar generalized their grievances into what became the standard view of the spoliation of the church.[15] In the eighth century, however, ecclesiastical assemblies seem to have accepted the policy in principle, however reluctantly and as a tem-

13. Ibid., no. 138, c. 29; Goffart, *Le Mans Forgeries*, 6–20; on restorations see, e.g., *Urkunden Lothars I*, no. 40; Schiaparelli, *Diplomi di Berengario I*, nos. 47, 90, 100, 101; Cipolla, *Codice Diplomatico di Bobbio*, 1, no. 66; Lesne, *Histoire de la propriété ecclésiastique*, vol. 2, pt. 1.
14. Reynolds, *Fiefs and Vassals*, 89–100, 172–76.
15. Fouracre, *Age of Charles Martel*, 123–25.

porary expedient, because of the needs of the *res publica*.[16] *Res publica* sometimes meant only the king's own land and resources, but the words could have much wider connotations.[17] Particular words are in any case less important than the ideas behind them: *res publica* was sometimes used as a synonym for "kingdom" (*regnum*), which surely had connotations of collectivity and mutual obligations between king and subjects. The more frequent occurrence of words like *res publica* and *communis utilitas* in the writings of learned Carolingian clergy need not mean that the ideas they represent were being revived after a long post-Roman eclipse.[18] Whatever words were used, a king was supposed to employ his resources for the defense of his kingdom, and that emphatically included the defense of the clergy and their churches. The Merovingian kingdom, however often divided, had remained a single political community partly at least because its great men wanted it to remain and seems to have been managed by much the same hierarchical but collective institutions and responsibilities as was its Carolingian successor.[19]

Similar assumptions about collective interests and responsibilities, however often overridden by private interests in practice, seem, moreover, to be discernible in other kingdoms where kings

---

16. *Concilia Aevi Karolini*, no. 56, c. 59, of 836, reads: *Monasteria divinis solummodo cultibus dicata non debent et secularibus dari et canonica prodit auctoritas et ipsorum destructio locorum. Sed quia id exigit rei publicae necessitas, saltem conlapsa loca erigi debent et clerici locis, in quibus fuerant, restitui quousque oportunitas id permittit emendari plenius.* Wehlen, *Geschichtsschreibung*, 40, interprets this as meaning that monasteries were to be rebuilt *quia id exigit rei publicae necessitas*, but the needs of the *res publica* seem more likely here to justify the giving of them to laymen, as in *Capitularia*, 2, no. 227, c. 5, of 844, and the taking of some land in *Codice Diplomatico di Bobbio*, no. 66, of 877.

17. Janet Nelson, "Kingship and Empire," 227. On the range of uses: Wehlen, *Geschichtsschreibung*; Goetz, "Regnum."

18. Hibst, *Utilitas Publica*, esp. 156–61.

19. Murray, "From Roman to Frankish Gaul"; Fouracre, "Carolingian Justice."

took or borrowed land from churches. In 915, when a house of the bishop of Pavia had been demolished for a new city wall, King Berengar gave him permission to build one on top of the wall and to have the line of the wall and of a road diverted for his convenience. Other Italian bishops received royal license to build or repair town defenses. This may not have involved any expropriation, since the walls in some cases were said to have been hitherto part of the king's *res publica*, which now passed to the bishop.[20]

English kings who took church lands for themselves or their servants in the ninth and tenth centuries could have justified doing so by needs of defense just as well as did the Carolingians.[21] Some of what they took they acquired by exchange, which obviated the need to pay compensation or to promise that the lands would be returned to the church. Although churches were not supposed to alienate the property of God and the saints, exchange did not count as alienation. Some of the many exchanges of land between rulers and churches may therefore have been made in order to compensate churches for lands which rulers had taken for what they claimed was the common good. One example of this could be the grant of land at Saint-James-de-Beuvron (Manche) that William the Conqueror made to Saint-Benoît-sur-Loire (Loiret) in 1067 in exchange for what he had apparently taken from them to build a fortification for the defense of his land (*ob mee terre defensionem*): "his land" here probably means the territory he ruled and its inhabitants, rather than his own immediate property.[22] More surprisingly, perhaps, Domesday Book records that William also compensated the archbishop of Canterbury and St. Augustine's abbey for land he had taken for the castle at Canterbury, and the bishop of Rochester for land taken there for a cas-

20. Schiaparelli, *Diplomi di Berengario I*, nos. 47, 90, 100, and also 137 (a marquis's fortifications on his own land); Schiaparelli, *Diplomi di Ugo e di Lotario*, no. 11.
21. Dumville, *Wessex and England*, 29–54; Reynolds, *Fiefs and Vassals*, 329.
22. Bates, *Regesta Regum Anglo-Normannorum*, no. 251.

tle, all by exchanging other land for what he had taken.²³ He also gave Westminster Abbey the manor of Battersea in exchange for Windsor, and Shaftesbury Abbey a church in exchange for what he took for Corfe Castle (Dorset).²⁴ That does not, of course, mean that he compensated all churches for what he took from them for castle building,²⁵ but similar exchanges with churches by two of his greater followers are recorded: Robert of Mortain gave two manors to the bishop of Exeter in exchange for a castle in Cornwall (presumably Launceston) and William Fitzosbern gave the bishop of Hereford a manor in exchange for land he took for a market (presumably in Hereford).²⁶ There may be other cases that were not recorded or that I have missed, but even these few suggest the pressure of norms even on conquerors in occupied territory.

2.4 FORTIFICATIONS

If the needs of defense and the public good could justify the taking or borrowing of church land, they presumably also justified, and more easily, the taking of land from laymen. Some new fortifications around existing settlements followed the line of older defenses, but others may not have done so, in which case bits of land may have been taken from individuals, some of whom may have held it as their own by hereditary right. Where there were older defenses, medieval townspeople were given to building on or next to them. According to the Roman jurist Ulpian this had needed authorization from the emperor or governor, but in early

---

23. *Domesday Book*, vol. 1, fols. 2r, 2v.
24. Ibid., fols. 32r, 78v. *Domesday* has Wareham rather than Corfe, but see Colvin, *History of the King's Works*, 2:852 n.
25. The bishop of Lincoln, for instance, was not apparently compensated for loss of a house *in loco castri* in Huntingdon: *Domesday Book*, vol. 1, fol. 203r.
26. Ibid., fols. 101v, 121v, 181v.

medieval conditions it probably often happened without any permission, and those who did it could have established some kind of rights by prescription.[27] Little is recorded about the building of most fortifications, but there are some occasions about which there is enough information at least to raise questions about the acquisition of the land on which walls, banks, or ditches were constructed.

In 848–52 a wall was built at Rome around St. Peter's and the settlement beside it on the right side of the Tiber. A similar project about fifty years earlier had been abandoned, so that the new wall may have run along the same line, but the growth of the settlement round St. Peter's presumably meant that, whether in 800 or 848, part at least of the line may have lain through private property. The new wall was named the Leonine Wall after Pope Leo IV, who summoned a great assembly of people from inside and outside Rome to organize the work, but the original initiative seems to have come from the Emperor Lothar. In 846 he had ordered money to be collected for the wall from the whole kingdom of Italy, presumably in the first instance from benefice holders, since he told the bishops of the kingdom to encourage those with allods or money to contribute as would those with benefices. He and his brothers, Charles the Bald and Louis the German, also made substantial contributions (*non modicas argenti libras*). Surviving inscriptions on the wall imply that different local communities built different sections.[28]

Some of the fortifications ordered by Charles the Bald in 864 *ad defensionem patriae* may have been repairs of old defenses, but others, or parts of them, may have been built on bits of land

---

27. Mommsen et al., *Corpus Iuris Civilis*, 1:26 (Digest I.8.9.4).
28. *Capitularia*, vol. 2, no. 203; Duchesne, *Liber Pontificalis*, 2:123–24, 137–38; Ginson and Ward-Perkins, "Surviving Remains of the Leonine Wall"; on ninth-century Italian benefices and allods: Reynolds, *Fiefs and Vassals*, 192–94, 198, 207.

that individuals had to give up.²⁹ The same goes for the defensive works organized by Mercian kings from the eighth century, by kings of Wessex from the ninth, and by Henry the Fowler in Saxony in the tenth.³⁰ Where archaeologists find evidence of houses or other buildings underneath the walls or banks of any of these fortifications but apparently dating from not long before them, that suggests that land may have had to be acquired from previous owners or occupiers in order to build at least part of the defenses.³¹ Nothing, however, seems to be recorded in France, Saxony, or England about the way it was acquired, whether for defensive works around existing settlements or for whole forts. Perhaps compensation was not thought to be due. However often individuals evaded their obligations or deserted from armies, the obligation of free men to defend both their local communities and the kingdom, or to supply provisions for those who did, seems to have been generally accepted. It could have covered the justice of giving up what were probably often small bits of land on which works for common defense would be built. Perhaps collective responsibilities, far from originating in the so-called communal movement of the twelfth century, were accepted even more easily before then, so that lay landowners gave up bits of land for communal fortifications without expecting compensation. Quite complex systems were prescribed for the rural soldiers (*agrarii milites*) of Saxony and the owners of specified amounts of land to share the work of building, provisioning, and guarding the forts there. The solidarities promoted by this, along with other local activities and responsibilities in government, probably allowed Henry the Fowler to assume that his *agrarii milites* would know

---

29. *Capitularia*, vol. 2, no. 273.

30. Hill, "Burghal Hidage"; Dumville, *Wessex and England*, 24–27; Widukind, *Rerum Gestarum Saxonicarum Libri Tres*, 48–49 (I. 35); Plummer and Earle, *Two Saxon Chronicles*, 1:84–87 (893).

31. E.g., at Hereford: Rahtz, "Archaeology of West Mercian Towns," 111, 126.

what he meant when he told them to hold their assemblies and feasts in the forts to which they were to give time and service. Some were perhaps also expected to give land without payment.

One case in which we can guess why compensation was apparently not made was that recorded in an agreement made in 1058 to build a wall round the north Italian village or town of Nonantola (Emilia-Romagna). The abbot undertook to build a quarter of the new wall while the inhabitants built the rest. He also gave them as a group all the land around the settlement within stated boundaries for their common good (*ad communem utilitatem suprascripti populi*) and promised not to grant any of it to anyone except for the common good of the people of Nonantola.[32] Here compensation for any land that was taken from individuals may have seemed inappropriate: everyone was supposed to contribute to the work and profit from it.

2.5 OTHER PROBABLE EXPROPRIATIONS

The same may apply to other expropriations which could, I suspect, have been made by local communities acting on their own initiative — which probably means that of the most prosperous and respected men among them — without formal approval from king or lord. So far, I have no direct evidence of this, but there is evidence here and there of collective local control of land use that could perhaps have involved the right to take bits of land from members of the community. From the sixth century Frankish laws gave the existing inhabitants of settlements the right to forbid newcomers to settle.[33] This may or may not have involved the allocation of rights over land. In 844 Charles the Bald allowed the Goths or Spaniards who had settled and made clearances (*aprisiones*) in the county of Barcelona to have control over their woods and pastures, with the right to make watercourses (*aquarum duc-*

---

32. Muratori, *Antiquitates*, vol. 3, cols. 241–43.
33. *Pactus Legis Salicae*, 172–76.

tus), all according to their old customs.³⁴ It is tempting to wonder whether making the watercourses involved expropriating bits of land. By the tenth and eleventh centuries there is evidence in various places that local communities exercised some sort of collective rights and controls over their use of woods and pastures.³⁵ It has been suggested that in some areas they may have reallocated arable holdings among their members, whether independently or under seigniorial pressure, though hard evidence seems to be lacking.³⁶ The relatively rich evidence from tenth-century northwest Spain shows local councils or assemblies (*concilia, collationes*) or other groups of local people giving and selling land, including cultivated land, and disputing with each other about the boundaries of their territories.³⁷ None of this proves that local communities could take land from their members for the common good, whether with compensation or not, but given the scarcity of evidence even about royal expropriations that seem very likely to have been made, it may be unreasonable to expect to find records of any that may have been made by peasant communities. That does not mean that there are no such records: they need to be looked for.

Apart from these suggestions of expropriation of relatively small bits of land from relatively unimportant lay people, I found one case from the late eleventh century that looks rather like expropriation from an important layman, compensated by an exchange of land. Presumably for reasons of defense (if not for fortifications, in the sense of walls or ditches) William the Conqueror divided the county of Sussex between five trusted followers who

---

34. Tessier et al., *Recueil des actes de Charles le Chauve*, vol. 1, no. 46; on *aprisiones* see Reynolds, *Fiefs and Vassals*, 108–10; Innes, *State and Society*, 108, 120–24.

35. Reynolds, *Kingdoms and Communities*, 111–12.

36. Rowley, *Origins of Open Field Agriculture*; Faith, *English Peasantry*, 219, 235–36; Fossier, *La terre et les hommes*, 335–36, 344 (though here the suggestion is, until later, rather of individual exchanges).

37. Davies, *Acts of Giving*, 198–207.

each held a length of the coast and the land behind it. At first there may have been only four of these lordships, known as rapes, but at some time between 1066 and 1086 the lord of the rape of Lewes surrendered part of his land to the lord of the rape of Pevensey, to the east of Lewes, and part to what may have been a new rape to the west. He received compensation for his losses in the form of extensive lands in Norfolk and Suffolk, described in Domesday Book as derived from "the exchange of Lewes" (*de escangio Lewes, pro escangio de Laquis*, etc.). The rearrangement may have been justified as providing for a better defense of the coast, and it may be that the property rights of the conquerors were still unsettled enough for adjustments to be easier than they would be later. Though there is no similar information about compensation for the lord of another rape, who also seems to have lost territory to the probably new rape, his acquisition of the county of Shropshire may have been partly designed to make up for his loss in Sussex.[38]

2.6 UNJUST EXPROPRIATIONS

While land was sometimes taken for what seemed the common good, whether with or without compensation, it was also sometimes said to have been taken unjustly, which casts further doubt on the suggestion that lords before the twelfth century were *allowed* to expropriate entirely at will.[39] I suggest that unjust expropriations were those thought not to have been made for the common good. That would include confiscations made for crimes that had not been committed, had been unjustly judged, or had not been judged at all. The abbot of Nonantola in his 1058 charter gave the men of the town various legal privileges and promised, among other things, not to seize their goods or demolish their

---

38. Mason, "Rapes of Sussex," with full references to *Domesday*; Hudson, "Origins of Steyning and Bramber," 18–19.

39. See chapter 2.2.

houses except as law commanded, saving his jurisdiction (*secundum quod lex precipit salva donnicata justitia*). This suggests that while he or his predecessors had sometimes taken property from them in the past as a punishment, and therefore without compensation, they thought that he or they had sometimes taken it arbitrarily and without due judgment or compensation, which they considered wrong. Either way, it suggests that the men of Nonantola had an idea about the rights and wrongs of a lord's taking of property from his subjects, and that the abbot, whether or not he would have agreed with it in the past, was now prepared to accept it — at least for the time being. Complaints made in tenth- and eleventh-century England about forced sales to churches, or the seizure of land by kings to give to churches, also imply norms that were allegedly being broken.[40] Suggestions of supposedly unlawful expropriations in the past are made in a charter granted by Emperor Henry IV to Lucca in 1081 and, slightly less clearly, in another in the same year to Pisa.[41] A Norman complained at William the Conqueror's funeral at Caen that William had unjustly seized land on which the church where the funeral was held had been built. He may not have had a good case but was nevertheless bought off, presumably to avoid trouble at what those at the funeral considered such an unfitting time.[42]

William had, of course, famously expropriated many important Englishmen, but that was on the ground, however specious, that they were rebels and traitors. As for English townspeople whose houses were demolished to make way for castles after the Conquest but who did not, like churches, get compensation for them, their losses no doubt seemed unjust to them. Townspeople who were not important enough to be worth counting

---

40. Blake, *Liber Eliensis*, 79–80, 83, 91, 109 (II.7, 10, 12, 34).

41. *Diplomata Regum et Imperatorum*, vol.6 (1), nos. 334, 336.

42. Orderic Vitalis, *Historia Ecclesiastica*, 4:106 (VII.16); William of Malmesbury, *Gesta Regum Anglorum*, 1:513 (III.283); Musset, *Actes de Guillaume*, nos. 14 (pp. 106, 107, 109, 110), 20 (pp. 127, 128).

as traitors were, however, presumably not important enough to object. It was, after all, a violent conquest, and they had to keep their heads down.[43] That kind of confiscation, though it could have been represented as done for the common good, lies outside my scope here. According to Henry of Huntingdon, William also had villages demolished and the inhabitants moved out to make hunting grounds, again presumably without compensation. That was thought to have been wrong, at least by Henry and, probably, other English people. If the allegation related to the New Forest, however, Domesday Book suggests that it may be wrong or exaggerated: settlement there may already have been sparse and not all of it, or all that was arable, is thought to have disappeared.[44]

2.7 CONCLUSION

Meager and at least partly uncertain as this evidence from before 1100 is, there is, I suggest, just enough of it to suggest that kings who took or borrowed land from churches thought that they were justified in doing so for what they saw as the common good of their kingdoms, and that they — or some of them — also believed they ought to make some sort of compensation. Evidence of lay collective activity, such as it is, suggests that these ideas about the common good could perhaps also have been used to justify local communities in taking land from individuals for the common good. I cannot claim to have proved that land was taken from laymen in the earlier Middle Ages for objects such as the building of fortifications that were deemed necessary for the common good, but I can, I hope, claim that there is just enough evidence to show that we cannot, at present, be sure that it was not. I have found no hint about compensation for land taken except what was paid to

---

43. Domesday Book records demolitions but no claims to compensation for them: Fleming, *Domesday Book and the Law*, index p. 526 (castles).
44. Henry of Huntingdon, *Historia Anglorum*, 404 (VI. 39); Finn, "Hampshire," 324–38.

churches and, thanks to the quite exceptional record of Domesday Book, to one or two fortunate Normans among the followers of William the Conqueror. I conclude tentatively that, though it is possible that compensation was paid to other laymen but not recorded, the common good may have been held to outweigh individual rights to the extent that compensation may not always have been thought necessary — except for land taken from God and the saints.

CHAPTER 3

Western Europe and British North America, 1100–1800

3.1 THE PLAN OF THE CHAPTER

I start my argument about the practice of expropriation for the common good after 1100 with England, because, after providing the evidence from Domesday Book that I cited in chapter 2.3 and 2.5 of compensation paid to churches and Norman invaders for lands taken from them, England then provides my next piece of reasonably hard evidence in 1130. I then take up Italy, where I discuss a case from 1156 that, though chronologically not the next, is nicely unambiguous and quickly followed by even better cases. It is not surprising that the best, as well as the earliest, medieval evidence comes from England and Italy, the two areas in which something like Weberian bureaucracy and record keeping developed first. Since the records are, in one case, those of the central government of a kingdom and, in the other, those of city-states, since the forms of their legal systems were quite different, and since the two areas were so far apart, the likelihood of influence flowing from one to the other in either direction is small. That makes the similarities in the way that expropriation worked in both countries all the more suggestive of norms that I suspect were already accepted throughout western Europe.

Some of the conclusions that I draw from those two countries may therefore help in the interpretation of the less full information about other areas that I then go on to consider. After Italy I discuss France, Germany (with Austria and the Netherlands),

Spain, and the English colonies in America, in that order. The section on France covers more or less the area within its modern boundaries, including one or two medieval cases that took place in areas that were not then part of the kingdom. With but a few cases from Austria and the Netherlands to consider, I put them into the section that deals mainly with Germany — an arrangement that would probably look more reasonable to a medievalist than to the citizens of any of the three modern states. The examples of expropriation in the countries I discuss are limited in number and content but are enough, I hope, to suggest both that expropriation for what was taken to be the public good was probably going on in all these countries throughout the period; and that it does not seem at any stage to have been an innovation derived from new kinds of law or new ideas of the public good.

3.2 ENGLAND

In England neither historians nor lawyers have shown much interest in the history of expropriation for the common good. English lawyers writing on property law have traditionally set out their work under long-hallowed headings that do not include it.[1] One

---

1. Blackstone (see below and chapter 4.3) and Bentham (*Theory of Legislation*, 144, 148) are exceptions. But Bacon, *New Abridgement*, for instance, with headings for "Approvement" (in which enclosure of commons is mentioned, with reference to the Statute of Merton) and for "Highways," has nothing about parliamentary authorization of expropriation for either. Williams, *Principles of the Law of Real Property*, does not mention expropriation, though the second edition (1849), 349, 403, in discussing more traditional subjects, mentions the Land Clauses Consolidation Act, 1845. Cheshire, *Modern Law of Real Property*, does not refer to it until a brief mention in the 8th edition (1958), 121–2, with fuller accounts from the 9th (1962), 853–59. On legal history, the index to Holdsworth, *History of English Law*, does not seem to include any entry that refers to anything about compulsory acquisition (e.g., under acquisition, conveyance, land, public law, or railways). More information comes from Clifford, *History of Private Bill Legislation*, 1:453, 470, 479–84.

standard work, published first in 1957, included passing references to it in its fourth edition eighteen years later, when it connected the procedure with twentieth-century higher taxes and "social control of land," which the authors perhaps considered a modern phenomenon.[2] American legal writers who have discussed the origins of eminent domain have provided some useful examples and arguments.[3] In spite of the relative lack of work on the subject, however, the abundance of records produced by the royal government in England has produced a fair amount of evidence about expropriation by kings from the twelfth century on.

My first case after 1100 does no more than confirm what was implied in Domesday Book (1086): that royal castles counted as buildings that, as seats of legitimate government, served the public good, so that the king felt an obligation to make compensation for land that he needed for them, at least if he took it from churches. In 1130 the first surviving Pipe Roll, or annual written account of royal income and expenditure, records that the sheriff of Northamptonshire paid 3s. 8d. to the monks of Northampton Abbey for their land which the king had taken into his castle in the town.[4] Not that the public good is actually mentioned in the brief entry in the Pipe Roll, any more than it is in many of the less cryptic references to expropriation both in England and elsewhere during the Middle Ages. It nevertheless seems to be assumed, if only by the combination of what looks like compulsory surrender of the land, the purpose for which it was to be used, and the assessment and award of compensation.

According to the life of St. Hugh of Lincoln, Henry II gave a

---

2. Megarry and Wade, *Law of Real Property*, 4th ed. (1975), 775, 1104. The 6th edition (2001), by C. Harpum, is fuller, though with no historical background, in contrast to the traditional account of tenures, etc., at the beginning of the book.

3. See especially Stoebuck, "General Theory," even if I contest some of his points below.

4. *Pipe Roll 31 Henry I*, 135. This and later references were found through the index in Colvin, *History of the King's Works*, vol. 2, under "compensation."

royal estate at Witham (Somerset) to the Carthusian monastery that he founded there about 1178–80, evicting the peasants who lived there. Hugh, who was the first abbot, interceded for them with the king so that they were offered houses and land on any royal manor they chose or were allowed to go where they wanted, absolved from their former services or servitude (*pristine servitutis iugo absoluti*). Hugh also insisted that the king should compensate them for their houses and improvements. The peasants were delighted with this new method of arranging their dealings with the king (*novo negotionis genere exhilarati*).[5] That Hugh did not object to the taking as such could be because he was interested only in the prospects of his monastery but, like Henry and his contemporaries in general, he presumably assumed that monasteries served the public good. The hagiographical context, together with the reference to novelty, would make the contemporary recognition of a norm slightly doubtful if it were not for the Pipe Roll evidence from Henry's reign. Hugh may have been making the king do what was generally agreed to be right, though whether the norm applied to land taken from people of such low status is doubtful. The Witham peasants would not, presumably, have been covered by the prohibition in clause 39 of Magna Carta (1215) against the arbitrary seizure of land from free men. That clause nevertheless suggests that kings of England, or at least King John, were thought to have taken land wrongly and against custom.[6] The Pipe Rolls show that they sometimes compensated those from whom they took land, but they may well not have done so every time.

The Pipe Rolls of 1169 and 1174 show that by then, if not before, the king or his officials recognized an obligation to compensate lay people, even if we may suspect that the obligation was not always fulfilled. The 1169 case records compensation paid to a laywoman for land taken for Canterbury Castle. That of 1174 may not have involved the taking of actual land, as the money was paid to a

---

5. Adam of Eynsham, *Life of St. Hugh*, 46–47, 60–62.
6. Holt, *Magna Carta*, 326, 355 (cl. 29 in 1225 issue).

layman for his houses which were carried (*asportate*) into Orford Castle for the accommodation of the garrison.[7] Both these people were presumably of higher status than the Witham peasants, but neither seems to have had as high status as the Norman lords who Domesday Book shows were compensated by an exchange of land. At about this time the royal treasurer, explaining the way the exchequer worked, said that the cost of royal buildings was assessed by the view (*per visum*) of two or three men.[8] The same system probably often applied to compensation for land: there are examples in the first half of the thirteenth century that were to be assessed *per visum* or by the sworn testimony of worthy and lawful men (*proborum et legalium hominum*).[9] In Newcastle-on-Tyne the assessment of damages was left to the town authorities, who were told to pay those who had suffered losses as a result of the king's works there in proportion to the size of their losses.[10] In 1221 land taken for the barbican of Bridgnorth (Shropshire) Castle was compensated in land rather than in money. In at least some of these cases compensation was apparently paid several years after the land had been taken, and where it took the form of an annual rent, subsequent reminders were needed to get it paid.[11] In 1243 Henry III took the towns of Winchelsea and Rye (Sussex), with other coastal land, from Fécamp Abbey (Seine-Maritime) on the ground that the abbey could not defend them in time of war and granted it inland property in exchange.[12] When Edward I in 1280 ordered land to be surveyed and acquired by purchase or exchange for the foundation of New Winchelsea, the sales may well

---

7. Colvin, *History of the King's Works*, 2:588, 770. The reading *asportate* is taken from the chancellor's roll: *Pipe Roll 20 Henry II*, 38 and n.

8. Richard Fitz Nigel, *Dialogus de Scaccario*, 89–90.

9. *Calendar of the Liberate Rolls*, 1:396–97; 2:202; *Rotuli Litterarum Clausarum*, 1:481.

10. *Rotuli Chartarum*, 1:190.

11. *Rotuli Litterarum Clausarum*, 1:464; Colvin, *History of the King's Works*, 2:577 (other cases, ibid., 712, 716, 746, 757).

12. *Calendar of the Charter Rolls*, 1:321.

have been, in effect, compulsory.[13] In 1292 he made Meaux Abbey (Yorkshire) give up land on which he planned to establish the port of Hull (Kingston upon Hull, Yorkshire), though it then took about eighteen years of complaints before the abbey got what its chronicler considered more or less adequate compensation.[14]

All these cases probably counted as serving the general good, whether for the defense or prosperity of the kingdom or, in the case of Witham, by the foundation of a church. Whether contemporaries would have seen Edward's taking of Swainstone manor (Isle of Wight) plus £2,000 from the bishop of Winchester in that light is more doubtful. The compensation looks rather minimal: it consisted of the confirmation of the bishop's title to property that had long been in dispute between him and the prior of Winchester and a not very valuable franchise in part of it.[15] An occasional abuse or breach of a norm, as this seems to have been, does not, however, invalidate the argument that it was generally accepted.

Thirteenth-century kings took an active interest in the defenses of some towns, apart from the royal castles within them. This included some that had a measure of autonomy and that may sometimes have taken property for their fortifications on their own account. It seems, however, that the king could be regarded as responsible for making compensation, perhaps because he had ordered the town walls to be strengthened or repaired: it was consequently to him that complaints were made when property was taken and not paid for.[16] In one case, that was so even though the work was said to have been done for the good of the town

---

13. *Calendar of the Patent Rolls, 1272–1281*, 414; *1281–1292*, 3, 81–82; Inderwick, *Story of King Edward and New Winchelsea*, 218–19.

14. *Chronica monasterii de Melsa*, 2:186–92, 232.

15. Deedes, *Registrum Johannis de Pontissara*, xiii–xvi, 402, 422, 426–37, 719. Droxford, East Meon, and Havant already belonged to the church, whether the bishop or the prior: *Victoria History of Hampshire*, 3:65, 122–23, 284–85.

16. *Calendar of Inquisitions Miscellaneous*, vol. 1, nos. 338, 379, 1087.

(*ad munitionem et utilitatem totius civitatis*), as well, presumably, as for the defense of the kingdom. Three complaints, from 1267, 1277, and 1308, that land had been taken without compensation resulted in royal orders to hold an inquiry. The taking of the land and the loss sustained were then certified by sworn juries of twelve (or in one case, fourteen) worthy and lawful men.[17] That two of the three complaints I found came from churches can be explained by the likelihood that kings would pay more attention to them than to ordinary townspeople. In 1305, when a road along the Humber had been washed away to the great injury of the local community (*la comunalte de pays*), it was the prior of Bridlington (Yorkshire) who petitioned the king, on behalf, he said, of that community, as well as of his priory. He asked that a new road be made, compensating the owners of land that would be taken.[18] One lay person secured compensation from the king for land on the site of New Winchelsea by a belated exchange: he was the guardian of a minor who was presumably of high enough status to be able to persist in getting his due.[19] Not all who were compensated, however, were important people, and not all compensation needed special petitions: in 1239 over £160 was paid out for land taken for the enlargement of the Tower of London to nearly fifty individuals, including apparently humble lay people as well as the heads of religious houses and a parish priest. The worthy and lawful men who assessed their losses evidently valued each house or plot separately.[20] The taking of property from Jews, when they were expelled in 1290, needed no compensation, because it was presented as punishment for their having persisted in usury after

17. Inquisitions on land taken at Gloucester (1267), Hereford (1277), Winchelsea (1308): Chancery inquisitions miscellaneous, C 145/14/16, 35/31, 68/24, National Archives, London.

18. Maitland, *Memoranda de Parliamento*, 32–33.

19. *Calendar of Inquisitions Miscellaneous*, vol. 2, no. 24; Chancery inquisitions miscellaneous, C 145/68/24, National Archives, London.

20. Colvin, *History of the King's Works*, 2:716; *Calendar of the Liberate Rolls*, 1:396–97.

it had been forbidden, as well as being to the honor of God and the good (*ad utilitatem*) of the king's people.²¹

By the later Middle Ages, churches were becoming more vulnerable to more permanent and absolute seizures, without exchange or compensation, than they had been earlier. Lands in England belonging to French churches were confiscated when the two kingdoms were at war. In 1414 a parliamentary petition of the Commons that this confiscation become permanent was granted for the peace and common good ("la commune profit") as well of the church as of the whole kingdom.²² No compensation was presumably needed because the owners of the lands were French and therefore enemies. All these seizures created useful precedents for the dissolution of the monasteries, which also needed no compensation since the communities that had owned property no longer existed.

I have found no examples of expropriation by lesser lords in England but, though most of them had fewer and less independent rights of jurisdiction than had lords in other kingdoms and were more closely supervised by the royal government, some may have exercised the same right to expropriate as lords probably did elsewhere. That they were not supposed to take land arbitrarily is clear from the procedures introduced in the twelfth century to deal with unjust *disseisin* (i.e., taking of land), which may have been particularly directed against lords. As for the taking of land by towns (as distinct from the takings by kings for town defenses), I have found only a few cases, all after 1300, though I suspect that this is not because they did not happen earlier.²³ Because fortification in England was in principle under royal control, towns

---

21. Rigg, *Select Pleas*, xl–xli.

22. *Rotuli Parliamentorum*, 4:22; New, *History of Alien Priories*.

23. On Newcastle see *Calendar of the Close Rolls, 1318–1322*, 54, though *Calendar of the Patent Rolls, 1301–1307*, 105, may be the result of building at royal command. M. D. Harris, *Coventry Leet Book*, 142–43, 447, 463. On Sandwich see *Black Book of Sandwich*, fol. 223 (bricks given for an indi-

sometimes got royal permission to build walls or take tolls to pay for them, but the right to take land for the fortifications is very seldom mentioned. That may have been because it was taken for granted.[24] In 1240 the town of Bristol bought land by normal, apparently unforced, negotiations with the religious house that owned it in order to make a new channel to improve their harbor. The king told the men of neighboring Redcliffe to help Bristol with this for the common good (*pro communi utilitate*) of both communities.[25] I have found no evidence to suggest that position in the "feudal hierarchy" affected vulnerability to expropriation in England. Status no doubt made a difference (despite the lucky peasants of Witham), and the conditions on which land was held may have affected the compensation, but I have not found evidence that land held on any free tenures or any particular levels in the hierarchy of lordship was more, or less, subject to expropriation than any other.

From the sixteenth century, expropriation was increasingly authorized by acts of parliament. By the eighteenth century, Blackstone thought an Englishman's "absolute right" to property could be overruled only by an act of "the legislature . . . an exercise of power, which the legislature indulges with caution, and which nothing but the legislature can perform."[26] The need for an act of parliament does not seem to have been the effect of any formal legislation but part of a development of centralized control that can also be found in other European polities. Where Roman

---

vidual's garden wall as compensation for land taken for town wall, 1475), East Kent Archive Centre.

24. Ballard and Tait, *British Borough Charters*, 120–21, 377; *Calendar of the Patent Rolls, 1413–1416*, 224, 368–69, where the king was clearly concerned because of coastal defenses; *Calendar of Patent Rolls, 1429–1436*, 57–58, maybe because this involved a church.

25. *Elenchus*, vol. 2(2): England, no. 73. Nos. 62 and 66 make reference to *communis utilitas*.

26. Blackstone, *Commentaries*, 1:138–39 (I.1).

law was becoming increasingly dominant, the general assumption that the right to expropriate was reserved to sovereign rulers may have been influenced by the discussions of expropriation among academic Roman lawyers, which had generally focused on the emperor's right to expropriate.[27] That, however, does not seem to explain the similar assumption in England: perhaps, both in England and elsewhere, it was the effect of governmental practice rather than of legal principles or theories. Although local justices of the peace are sometimes said to have kept local government in England more independent than it became in countries where the theory and practice of cameral government were developed, the gradual development of parliamentary control brought about a rather similar assumption: that expropriation was a matter for the central, sovereign authority.

The dissolution of the monasteries presumably formed a powerful precedent for this, but it was only gradually that parliamentary sanction came to be generally accepted as necessary in the way that Blackstone assumed. The evidence of earlier expropriations rules out the suggestion that the practice of it in England started with parliament. Despite some seventeenth-century arguments about Magna Carta, there does not seem to have been any significant difference between the taking of land, with compensation, by parliament or by royal prerogative.[28] Purveyance was a royal right, but it covered only the taking of goods, materials, and labor, not the taking of land. Land needed by the government for dockyards or other defenses in the sixteenth century and later was sometimes acquired by leases or purchases negotiated without apparent compulsion.[29] When there was compulsion, it was not always authorized by act of parliament, any more than it had been in past centuries. In 1527 the eleven owners of small pieces

---

27. See chapter 4.2.
28. As suggested by Stoebuck, "General Theory," 562–66.
29. Oppenheim, "Royal Dockyards," 337–40, 344, 346, 351, 354–55, 359–60, 366.

of ground at Portsmouth, which together came to only nine acres, were presumably compelled to sell them in the traditional way, though the valuations in this case were made by two royal officials rather than the traditional local men. Land in Kent acquired in 1559–68 for the building of Upnor Castle was valued by six "indifferent persons," which may also imply compulsion.[30] Work on rivers that might involve taking land was, however, authorized in 1515 and 1539 by acts of parliament that each provided for compensation.[31] In 1585 an act authorized the mayor and citizens of Chichester (Sussex) to take land to improve their harbor. What they took was to be valued by a panel of four aldermen of the town and eight noblemen or gentlemen in the county commission of the peace.[32] Acts of parliament were quickly passed in 1667 after the Great Fire of London the year before, allowing the city to acquire land to widen streets and to pay for it out of new duties on coal. Since some thirteen thousand houses had been destroyed and their titles and tenancies were often very complicated, special Fire Courts were set up to adjudicate disputes, with appeals from them to the Court of Aldermen.[33]

Roads were often a matter for legislation, but the early acts

---

30. Accounts for the king's works at Portsmouth (1527): State Papers of Henry VIII, SP 1/45, fols. 179–80 in MS foliation, fols. 175–76 in printed foliation; and for land acquired at Upnor (1568): Pipe Office, declared accounts, E 351/2204, m [3d], both in National Archives, London.

31. Act concerning the river in Canterbury: 6 Henry VIII, c. 17; Act for mending the river at Exeter: 31 Henry VIII, c. 4, in *Statutes of the Realm*, 3:134–35, 720.

32. Rastell, *Collection*: 27 Eliz., c. 22; Clifford, *History of Private Bill Legislation*, 1:470, 479, 480–84. Some earlier acts mentioned by Stoebuck, "General Theory", 565, 575–79, involved the taking of materials, etc., not actual expropriation of land. The first act clearly taking land for roads that I have found is Act for enlarging and repairing of common highways: 14 Chas. II, c. 6, §5, in *Statutes of the Realm*, 5:375; Webb and Webb, *English Local Government*, 165–72.

33. See 18 & 19 Charles II, c. 7–8, in *Statutes of the Realm*, 5:601–12; Reddaway, *Rebuilding of London*, 72–100, 142–44, 155–64.

were concerned with enforcing the obligation of parishes to repair their roads rather than with widening or straightening them, let alone laying out new ones. The acts might authorize the taking of materials for roads, or even digging ditches beside them, without compensation, but that seems to have been customary and did not deprive landowners of their title.[34] An act passed in 1662 allowed the taking of land to improve a road but required it to be done with the owner's consent as well as compensation.[35] Turnpike acts were at first equally restricted in their aims. An act of 1723 that provided for the taking of land referred the assessment of damages, if the owner and tenants would not agree to what was proposed, to a sworn jury of twelve indifferent men of the parish or adjoining parishes. By the mid-eighteenth century, many turnpike trusts were given the power to buy land and divert roads. The compensation, if not agreed upon, was to be decided by a jury.[36] By then canals were also being built, whether by wayleave (easement) or, more often, under acts of parliament that provided for the taking of land. Occasionally, in the face of fierce opposition, the land could be obtained only by paying more than the formal valuation.[37]

The greatest number of expropriations in early modern England were those made for the enclosure of open fields and commons. Although often not represented as expropriation, enclosures of open fields extinguished rights in particular pieces of land just as much as if compensation had been made in money rather than by other land. Enclosures were at first made by local agreements, but

34. See, e.g., Acts for amendment of highways: 5 Eliz., c. 13, §§2–3; 15 Charles II, c. 1, §4; 3 Wm. and Mary, c. 12, §12, in *Statutes of the Realm*, 4:441–43; 5:436; 6:318; Albert, *Turnpike Road System*.

35. 14 Charles II, c. 6, §5, in *Statutes of the Realm*, 5:375.

36. Act for repairing and widening a road in Hertfordshire: Public Acts 9 Geo. I, 443–44, House of Lords Record Office, London; Albert, *Turnpike Road System*, 14–22, 59, 201–13.

37. *Oxford Dictionary of National Biography*, 17:991–93, s.v. Egerton, Francis, third duke of Bridgewater; Malet, *Bridgewater*, 121–29.

they were often promoted primarily by larger landowners who wanted to profit from new agricultural methods and could get professional lawyers to argue their cases. Those who held land in the open fields got other land in exchange for what they lost, but this generally left smallholders and cottagers, who before enclosure had rights of common but little or no arable land, with virtually no compensation. Enclosures thus pitted landowners, and especially larger landowners, against the landless or smallholders in a different way from the kind of expropriations for fortifications or roads that involved taking small pieces of land from anyone who happened to have them along a line where works were planned. This did not mean that old ideas of the public good were ignored or overturned. In 1664 a chancery decree in a disputed case remarked that "it should not be in the power of one or two wilfull persons to oppose a publick good."[38] In an age of what was seen by landowners as agricultural improvement, the improvers assumed that, since landowners would be automatically compensated by land that they could improve more easily, it would all be for the general good. The representative "good men" who had ruled on compensations in the Middle Ages had always been the more prosperous of the community, but their interests in expropriations had not then been so inevitably opposed to those of the poor as they now became. From 1710 enclosures were increasingly made by acts of parliament, which soon came to be assumed to be essential. If the acts did not generally invoke the common good, that was probably more because the procedures and terminology of parliament and the common law had changed than because it was not thought to matter.[39]

It was, above all, the railways, after the period with which I am concerned, that provoked a rush of expropriation which brought

---

38. Holdsworth, *History of English Law*, 6:344 n.

39. Lambert, *Bills and Acts*, 133–34; Thompson, *Making of the English Working Class*, 237, and *Customs in Common*, 97–184; cf. Bentham, *Theory of Legislation*, 144.

both it and compensation into the courts in a big way. There was, however, as I have shown, nothing new either about expropriation or about compensation. Some early statutes, together with a case of 1792, have been cited to show that compensation was not yet normally due, but this seems to be explicable on the ground that neither the statutes nor the case cited authorized the taking of actual land.[40] At first, like some canals before them, railways were sometimes constructed on land made available by wayleave, but private acts of parliament were soon used to acquire freehold title, though it was not until 1845 that an act was passed to lay down a regular procedure for adjudicating compensation.[41]

3.3 ITALY

There is more secondary work on expropriation in Italy than in England. The authors of works on architecture and town planning in medieval and Renaissance Italy are, unsurprisingly, more interested in the buildings than in the way land for them was acquired, but two works provide an excellent guide to medieval expropriation in Italy: Ugo Nicolini's *La proprietà, il principe e l'espropriazione per pubblica utilità: Studi sulla dottrina giuridica intermedia*, as its title suggests, is focused more on doctrine than on the records of practice, but Pertile's *Storia del diritto italiano* (1892–1903) cites a good many statutes and other records. His references are exceptionally abbreviated, even by the standards of his time, but where I could not find his sources I have cited his notes. Apart from one date among those I could check, they seem very accurate.[42]

---

40. Stoebuck, "General Theory," 575–79; Treanor, "Origins," 697 n. and "Original Understanding," 786 n.

41. Land Clauses Consolidation Act, 8 Vict., c. 18, in Cripps, *Treatise on ... the Law of Compensation*, 229–81; Simmonds and Biddle, *Oxford Companion*, 67–68, 250–52, 364.

42. Pertile, *Storia*, 4:354–62.

My first example of expropriation with compensation, and implicitly for the common good, comes (through Pertile) from Genoa in 1156. In that year two men recorded their receipt and sharing of the price of some land in which they had both had interests and which the consuls had taken for the towers and walls of the city.[43] Then at Pisa in 1164 the oaths to be taken by incoming consuls included an undertaking that they would have any losses to landowners caused by the making of new ditches, walls, and roads assessed on oath, taking into account any compensating profit (*computato proficuo quod inde habetur*), acquired presumably by access to the new roads. They would also make new roads through any allod or other possession only after advice from all or the greater part of the senators. Compensation was to be paid to the owner or occupier (*dominus vel possessor*) and assessed by two discreet men, taking into account any compensating profit.[44]

The Pisans had by this time started to make extensive and well-informed use of Roman law in their courts,[45] so that they could have got ideas about expropriation from the few references to it in Justinian. But that seems improbable, given the Genoese case a few years before, quite apart from the earlier cases in England. The required consultation, even though those to be consulted were called senators, also looks traditional, and so do the valuations by two discreet men. The lack of any reference, for instance, to the *reipublicae utilitas* or *communis commoditas* mentioned in Justinian's edict about expropriation may also be significant.[46] The efflorescence of urban life and independent government in eleventh- and twelfth-century Italy not only created new needs for public works and led to the production of more records but may have stimulated thought and activity about ways of promot-

---

43. *Monumenta Historiae Patriae*, vol. 6: *Chartarum*, 2, nos. 288–89; Heers, "Porta aurea à Genes."
44. Bonaini, *Statuti*, 1:36, 37, 39.
45. Wickham, *Courts and Conflict*, 108–67.
46. Mommsen et al., *Corpus Iuris Civilis*, 3:53.

ing the common good. Collective government was, however, not in itself new and surely involved some kind of idea of the common good.[47] From the twelfth century on, the idea came to be better articulated and expressed, but it did not need to be discovered in Roman law and propagated to twelfth-century people, whether in town or country, in Italy or northern Europe. However narrowly or unfairly by democratic standards the good of any community was envisaged, it was about in the air. It was what roads and fortifications were supposed to serve and assumed to serve, provided those in charge of making them could be made to do their job honestly and not for their own profit. The taking of little bits of land from different people where they were required for walls or roads must have involved some degree of compulsion, but it is not clear that it involved new norms or rules or that it aroused much controversy. The Pisan oaths suggest that it merely needed regulation.

The same applied when the commune of Piacenza (Emilia-Romagna) acquired a piece of land in the Piazza del Duomo in 1179: the sale looks like another example of one that, if not exactly compulsory, was required for what was thought of as the common good.[48] In 1204 the commune of Vercelli (Piemonte) acquired land on which to build communal mills at a price fixed by its appraisers (here *estimatores comunis*, but more often *extimatores*).[49] As in later cases in Italian communes that mention a just price or valuations by neighbors or *extimatores*, this was surely not an entirely voluntary sale, which would have been negotiated between the parties.[50] In a Parma statute of 1227 it was ordained that, if

47. See chapter 5.2.1.
48. Falcone and Peveri, *Il registrum magnum di Piacenza*, vol. 1, no. 206.
49. Mandelli, *Il comune di Vercelli*, 2:36.
50. See, e.g., ibid., 3:156–57; Pertile, *Storia*, 4:357–58, 362 n.; Ugolino Nicolini, "Le mura medievali di Perugia," 718; Silvestrelli, "L'edilizia pubblica del comune di Perugia," 485, 488–89, 520–21. For the duties of communal *extimatores*: Muratori, *Antiquitates*, vol. 2, cols. 339–44; Fratri, *Statuti di Bologna*, 1:139–45.

neighbors wanted a *porticus* built before someone's house so that people could gather there, they could make him sell the land for it at a just price, after valuation by two good men. All those who would benefit from the *porticus* had to contribute to the cost.[51] In 1228 Milan was engaged in extensive town planning, with a new *palazzo comunale, piazza*, and streets radiating out from it, which must have involved a good many more or less compulsory sales by landowners.[52] The purchase of all the mills in Reggio nell'Emilia by the commune, recorded in deeds nearly all drawn up in two months of 1241, must have involved some compulsion.[53] It seems to have been the result of an ordinance and valuation made in the previous year.[54] In 1249, when Piacenza needed new fortifications and had a ditch made across the garden (*viridarium*) of the abbey of San Savino, the monks appealed to the pope, who said that they should have their property restored, but it is not clear that it was.[55]

By 1262, when various orders made then and earlier in Siena were collected together, the city seems to have had a fairly regular system of buying land that was needed for improving roads and

51. Roncini, *Statuta communis Parmae*, 1:98–9.

52. Baroni, *Atti del comune di Milano*, vol. 2, no. 219. The site of the new palazzo had presumably been taken earlier as there are references to meetings in the *novum palatium* from 1213: Manaresi, *Atti del comune di Milano*, no. 316. The 1228 document (though it may have been written earlier) also refers to one of the parcels purchased as being where the podestà's chapel now is.

53. Gatta, *Liber grossus*, vol. 3, nos. 279–329; Dussaix, "Les moulins à Reggio."

54. See, e.g., Gatta, *Liber grossus*, vol. 3, no 286: properties as they were at the time of the sentence (*sententie*) and valuation (*exstimationis*) issued by Gerardo de Corrigia when he was *podestà* of Reggio and similar references in others, though not in nos. 293–99, 322–24, 326–29, which were held in fief. For the date, see ibid., vol. 1, nos. 113–14.

55. Campi, *Dell'historia ecclesiastica di Piacenza*, 3:400. The building of mills by the commune on the monastery's property had been negotiated in 1180: see Falcone and Peveri, *Il registrum magnum di Piacenza*, vol. 1, no. 43.

water supplies or for building mills. The acquisitions and works seem to have been authorized in general terms by the commune, but the expenses, along with most of the detailed decisions, were largely left to the immediate neighbors, with those who stood to profit most paying most. In the entries I have noted, the land to be bought was generally valued by two or three good men of the neighborhood:[56] explicit mention of compulsion seems to be rare, presumably because public opinion brought most landowners into line.[57] There is no reference to anything like *communis utilitas*: the only *utilitas* mentioned is that of individuals.[58] What was agreed by all or most of those affected was, it seems, taken for granted as being for the common good. The commune of Bologna acquired many small bits of land at different dates throughout the thirteenth century in order to form the Piazza Maggiore, build a new *palazzo comunale*, straighten streets, and so on.[59] Some of them came from confiscations of the property of losers in political conflicts, but most were bought at the valuation of neighbors or the commune's *extimatores*, though at least two vendors succeeded in pushing up the price they received.[60] As in Siena, work that would particularly profit neighbors was sometimes to be done by them or at their expense, while the purpose of serving the public good may have been more often assumed than stated.[61]

---

56. Zdekauer, *Constituto del comune di Siena*, 186–88 (I.510–12), 294–95, 304–5, 312 n. 1, 330 n. 1, 338, 340–41, 223, 257 (III.70–74, 98–99, 121, 182, 206, 217, 223, 257).

57. Though it is mentioned in the rubric to ibid., III.257 (p. 353), and perhaps hinted at in p. 330 n.1 (a later addition).

58. See, e.g., ibid., 304–5, 312 (III.99, 121).

59. Bocchi, *Atlante*, 2:11–14, 25, 27, 75, 95–98; Fratri, *Statuti di Bologna*, e.g., 2:139–41; Fasoli and Sella, *Statuti di Bologna*, 2:170.

60. Bocchi, *Atlante*, 2:97–98; for the duties of *extimatores*: Fratri, *Statuti di Bologna*, 1:139–46; Fasoli and Sella, *Statuti di Bologna*, 1:66–70.

61. Even if the documents cited by Bocchi, *Atlante*, 14, 75, 97–98, which I have not seen, do not mention the public good, she is surely right in deducing that expropriation for the public good was an accepted procedure.

A new road in the village of Padulle in Bologna's *contado*, however, was explicitly intended for the common and public good (*pro comuni et publica utilitate*) of all the men of Padulle, and was to be made at the expense of all the inhabitants, free and unfree (*tam servorum quam liberorum*). An exchange of land, by permission of the bishop, with a parish church in the city was made for the good (*ad utilitatem et in utilitatem*) of the city of Bologna, while the improvement of a road to the Dominican friary was done in honor of God and St. Dominic (*in honorem et reverentiam Dei et beati Dominici fratrum predicatorum*), which implied the same thing.[62]

The taking of small bits of land for roads or walls is easy enough to characterize as expropriation and, in the terms of the time, for the common good. So is the acquisition of watercourses or land on which to put wells or fountains for the city's water supply, and even perhaps the takeover of mills that might grind its corn. Communes also, of course, made purchases by the usual sort of negotiation, without compulsion. Some acquisitions, notably of larger properties, were the result of political negotiations and compromises with more or less independent lords in the countryside, rather than applications of anything like an accepted right to expropriate.[63] The uncertainty about classifying some transactions as compulsory or not serves, in effect, as confirmation that expropriation (with compensation), however much resented in individual cases, conformed in principle to generally accepted norms. The city statutes that I have seen deal at most with procedures, not with the principle, which did not apparently need to be justified. Furthermore, I suggest more tentatively that though academic arguments about expropriation owed much to Roman law,[64] there is no clear evidence that actual practice did so.

Not that everything can have been as harmonious, even apart

---

62. Fratri, *Statuti di Bologna*, 2:395; Hubert, *Der Palazzo comunale*, 163–64.
63. Balestracci, "La politica delle acque urbane."
64. See chapter 4.2.

from individually difficult cases, as all this may suggest. Leaving aside the confiscation of land from political enemies of any current regime, which I have excluded but which could have been justified, however disingenuously, as being for the common good, the common good sometimes looks less common than it does in the case of city walls or roads.[65] The beautification of the city, which was increasingly often invoked as a reason for expropriation, could be used to favor the rich against the poor.[66] Procedures by which properties could be exchanged under the view of *extimatores* so as to consolidate inconveniently divided holdings (*ingrossatio*) may at first have been intended to deal equally between owners of large and small properties, but in the fifteenth century a royal ordinance for Sicily obliged people with small houses or holdings to sell them — though still at a just price — if they interfered with the building or enlargement of palaces that would embellish a city. In the sixteenth century there was apparently similar legislation in Savoy. By the eighteenth the privilege was being sufficiently abused in the Regno to be restricted, under regulation, to Palermo.[67]

Though others could surely produce more information about expropriation in the Italian countryside before the cities came under the control of rulers of larger territories, my sketchy searches have found virtually none in the Middle Ages, except when cities made improvements to roads or watercourses in their *contadi* or built fortifications in order to defend their borders.[68] I mention one episode, although it is perhaps at best of merely tangential

65. Crouzet-Pavan, "'Pour le bien commun'"; Heers, "En Italie centrale."
66. Pertile, *Storia*, 4:362; Fratri, *Statuti de Bologna*, 1:39; Betto, *Statuti di Treviso*, 588–9; Müntz, *Les arts à la cour des papes*, 182–87; *Constitutiones dominii Mediolanensis*, fol. 98v–99.
67. Muratori, *Antiquitates*, vol. 2, cols. 339–41; Fratri, *Statuti di Bologna*, 1:144; Orlando, *Un codice di leggi*, 143; Pertile, *Storia*, 4:359–62; Salvioli, *Trattato di storia del diritto italiano*, 530–31.
68. Pertile, *Storia*, 4:358; *Liber Iurium Reipublicae Genuensis*, 2, no. 257. Also perhaps for watercourses: Balestracci, "La politica delle acque urbane."

relevance, since it nevertheless suggests the difficulty of expropriating rights in land without compensation. Pope Innocent III founded a Charterhouse at Trisulti (Lazio), probably in 1204, and endowed it with the property of an abandoned abbey nearby. This caused trouble with neighboring communes, which claimed that the Carthusians were keeping them out of their accustomed pastures. Although the restriction of common rights did not constitute the full expropriation on which I am concentrating, rights of common counted as rights of property, so that it came near to it. After some years of remonstrating with the aggrieved communes, the pope had to give way to the extent of compensating one of them with rights in another pasture nearby. That turned out to create more trouble because the people of another of the communes in dispute with Trisulti said that the rights there belonged to them.[69] Although the common good might have been cited to justify expropriation for the foundation of a church, and although Carthusians, like Cistercians, sometimes evicted peasants from neighboring land, it may be that Innocent did not at first realize that his gifts to Trisulti meant taking the rights of others. When the monks of Trisulti first realized that parts of their property had been subject to common of pasture is unknown, but they then evidently hoped that the pope would back them up in resisting the claims against them, as indeed he did, though not very successfully.

A couple of examples of Italian legislation about expropriation and compensation between the sixteenth century and the end of eighteenth, along with references to others given in previous works, may suffice to suggest that it continued to take place under the various rulers of at least some parts of Italy. Apart from the Savoyard and Sicilian laws already mentioned, an ordinance of 1621, for instance, compelled landowners in a new quarter of Turin to sell their property, at valuation, unless they would build

69. Sechi, *La Certosa di Trisulti*, 24–27, 147–50, 156; Taglienti, *Il monastero di Trisulti*, 446–64.

on it themselves. Legislation for Austrian Lombardy in 1784 ordered that where the public good required, those who held land that was needed for new roads had to give it up, either at a price to which they agreed or at one fixed by the government engineer.[70]

3.4 FRANCE

I have already mentioned the suggestion of some French legal historians that expropriation started as an exercise of seignorial power.[71] According to this argument, the lord's original right was to expropriate in his own interest, and its surrender was the result of the weakening of seignorial power as the growth of municipal government and Roman law together promoted ideas of the common good.[72] Apart from what seems to me an unjustified assumption that ideas of the common good were in the air only from the twelfth or thirteenth century, the argument is weakened by relying, at least in the statements of it that I have seen, on evidence from the thirteenth century and later when, according to its proponents, seignorial power was being tamed. The history of expropriation in France after the Middle Ages, however, is usefully served by works on administrative history and law.

The first clear case of what looks like expropriation with compensation that I have found in France comes from 1197, when Richard I of England, acting as the duke of Normandy, acquired Les Andelys (Eure) from the reluctant archbishop of Rouen so as to build his great fortress of Chateau-Gaillard.[73] This, like other surrenders of land from churches to kings, may have been, in effect, compulsory, or at least hard to resist, and it was, apparently,

---

70. Pertile, *Storia*, 4:359–60, 362; Borelli, *Editti antichi e nuovi*, 929 (1621, c. 2); Bosio, *Della espropriazione*, 1:30–36. On the public good, see Mozzarelli, "'Pubblico bene.'"

71. See chapter 2.2, at n. 7.

72. Mestre, "Les origines seigneuriales" and "L'expropriation"; Harouel, "L'expropriation," esp. 43, and *Histoire*, 4–16.

73. Rymer, *Foedera*, 1:68.

only afterwards that Richard gave the archbishop other land in exchange. The exchange of land at Saint-Rémy-sur-Creuse (Vienne) that Richard, as the count of Poitou, had made with the abbey of Saint-Pierre de Maillezais (Vendée) in 1184 in order to build a fortress may also have been, in effect, compulsory.[74] Kings of France may have been acquiring land in similar ways before this. In 1189 or 1190 Philip Augustus referred to the taking of lands from St. Martin of Tours by his father, which he now compensated by an exchange. Another exchange made by Philip in 1190 has also been suggested as a possible expropriation.[75]

We come on to slightly clearer ground with Guillaume le Breton's account of the building of the walls of Paris by Philip Augustus in 1212. According to Guillaume, the king could by written law (*iure scripto*) build walls and ditches on others' property for the public benefit of the kingdom (*propter publicum regni commodum*). Philip, however, preferred equity to law and compensated those who suffered loss out of royal property (*de fisco proprio*).[76] Although Guillaume presented the compensation as exceptional and made by the king's generosity, it may have been what should have been paid by custom, even if not, in Guillaume's opinion, required under written (i.e., Roman) law.[77] Royal generosity may also, perhaps with more probability, explain the compensation paid by Louis IX to the dean and chapter of Saint-Laud, Angers, for houses taken and demolished for the royal castle there, but here too Louis may have been doing only what was generally thought right.[78] That seems to have been more obviously the case

---

74. Teulet et al., *Layettes*, vol. 1, no. 329; A. Richard, *Histoire des comtes de Poitou*, 2:230–31; Bardonnet, "Comptes et enquêtes," 39–56.

75. Delaborde et al., *Recueil des actes de Philippe Auguste*, vol. 1, nos. 269, 312; Leyte, *Domaine et domanialité*, 192 n.

76. Guillaume le Breton, *Gesta Philippi Augusti*, 241; Harouel, "L'expropriation."

77. For arguments among medieval Roman lawyers, see chapter 4.2.

78. Teulet et al., *Layettes*, vol. 4, no. 4792; cf. Leyte, *Domaine et domanialité*, 251–52.

when Philip IV had a large number of houses in Paris demolished to make way for a new palace. Royal commissioners took the land and assessed the compensation to be paid by way of rents, some to be paid to owners, some to occupiers, and apparently some to other people who had apparently been receiving rents from the properties. Some at least of the payments were made only after long delays.[79] Philip's seizure of the Templars' lands in 1307 strictly falls outside the scope of my enquiry, since he justified what he did by the crimes with which he charged them. The eventual transfer of most of the property of the order in France and elsewhere to the Hospitallers also makes its confiscation slightly different from taking and keeping land so that it could be used for the common good.[80]

From the thirteenth century there is also evidence of expropriations in France by other lords. Edward I of England, like Richard I, seems to have often, though not always, acquired what he needed in order to build or fortify *bastides* (new planned towns) in France by exchange with churches. Most of these exchanges seem to have left the owner of the land little option, so that they were, in effect, compulsory. As at Les Andelys, building sometimes started before the formalities were complete, though Edward was held up for three years in his purchase of the site of Sauveterre-de-Guyenne (Gironde) from a number of lay owners by a stubborn laywoman who did not want to sell her bit of it.[81] Other great lords seem to have claimed similar powers. Louis IX made his brother, Charles of Anjou, return land to someone who complained that he had not wanted to sell or exchange it with Charles.[82] This case, however, may be of marginal relevance since it is not clear that Charles had claimed to be acting for the general good. Beaumanoir held that the count of Clermont could take property that caused seri-

---

79. Borrelli de Serres, "L'agrandissement," 23–30, 51–53.
80. Barber, *Trial of the Templars*, 230–38.
81. Trabut-Cussac, "La fondation de Sauveterre-de-Guyenne."
82. Carolus-Barré, *Le procès de canonisation de Saint Louis*, 140–41 (c. 17).

ous nuisance (*nuise durement*) to his house or fortress or to the common good (*le commun pourfit*), though he had to make sufficient exchange if the owner would not sell. The count could also, as *souverain*, take land if a road needed to be moved, in which case the costs should be paid by those who made most use of the road.[83] The earliest versions of the customs of Anjou and Maine, which have been dated to c. 1300 or earlier, refer to a lord's right to take land from a customary tenant (*coustumier*) holding land from him to build a house in which to lodge (*se herberger*), dig a pond, or build a mill, giving compensation by a suitable exchange, presumably of land. It has been suggested that this was a survival of an older kind of expropriation in the lord's own interests,[84] but it could rather have been the result of the new demands and new legal arguments of the time. The three purposes could in any case have been brought within the requirement of being done for the general good, though they may, like anything to do with hunting rights, have been exceptions to it. Great lords, like Charles of Anjou, the count of Nevers, and Edward I of England as duke of Gascony, expelled Jews from their patches on their own initiatives before the expulsions from the whole kingdom that were ordered in 1306 and 1394. The taking of property from the expelled Jews could be justified either as punishment for the ritual murders that had long been alleged against them or simply as being done for the general good of the Christians of the kingdom.[85]

Lords of smaller local lordships may also have taken land from their subjects or tenants. Though occasions for doing so may have been most frequent in towns, and most likely to be recorded there, lords may well have got away more easily with taking it from

---

83. Beaumanoir, *Coutumes de Beauvaisis*, vol. 1, §730, vol. 2, §§1662–63, 1666. For the sense of *souverain* here, see §1662.

84. Mestre, "Les origines seigneuriales," 72–73, 77–78; Beautemps-Beaupré, *Coutumes de l'Anjou et du Maine*, 1:14–15, 20, 126 (§103); 2:525 (§1458); 3:lxi–lxv; *Établissements de Saint Louis*, 2:167.

85. Jordan, *French Monarchy and the Jews*, 30–31, 180–213, 250.

unfree rural tenants. Although lords, like kings, were, as I maintain, always supposed to rule in the interest of the community of their subjects, including the unfree, and to do so after consultation with representatives of the community and according to judgments made by them, the temptation to dispense with consultation of humble subjects must have been strong. It would be especially strong where there was no effective system of appeals to higher authority and no powerful subjects to challenge the lord's decisions in the way that great men could challenge a king's. How often lords either before or during the twelfth century wanted to take land from their subjects or tenants is unclear. If they did, and if, as has been argued, they thought they could do it arbitrarily, it has been suggested as part of that argument that their powers were tamed by concessions made in the charters that began to be granted to local communities in the twelfth century.[86] The twelfth century may have been a turning point insofar as it was perhaps only then that many local populations, whether in town or country, began to be big and rich enough to stand up to their lords and get their rights acknowledged and recorded. But although there is little direct evidence of expropriation, my reading of a good many charters, whether granted by kings or lesser lords, suggests that it was not a very live grievance. Charters to French towns before 1250 and a few to rural communities pay much attention to the regulation of legal procedures, subjecting them as far as possible to the judgment of members of the community. They regulate penal expropriations, which sometimes included the demolition of houses,[87] but only in the same way that they define and limit dues and services of all kinds.[88] While the charters may have been intended to prevent unjust penal expropriations for offences

---

86. Mestre, "Les origines seigneuriales"; Harouel, "L'expropriation."

87. See, e.g., *Elenchus*, vol. 2(1), nos. 22, 44, 65, 75, 79, 80, 83, 92–93, 96.

88. Prou, "Les coutumes de Lorris," 445–57; Verriest, "La fameuse charteloi de Prisches"; Teulet et al., *Layettes*, vol. 1, no. 314; Espinas, *Privilèges et chartes*, 1:4.

which had not been committed, the way that these punishments were mentioned in the charters implies that expropriation was not considered unjust if it was a punishment for a properly judged crime. If, moreover, it was thought that lords had been expropriating land by imposing unjust penalties, then that implies that they did not feel free to take their subjects' lands unless it was done under the color of punishment.

At least two charters refer to the responsibility of town governments for the building or repair of their walls,[89] but few that I have seen say anything about the acquisition of land for this or any other public purpose. One exception comes in the customs granted by the later Edward I of England to Bordeaux in 1261, which allowed him to take properties needed for works on the castle, paying prices agreed by worthy citizens.[90] Two others, though not strictly from within the kingdom of France, are charters granted to towns in the Dauphiné before it was absorbed into the kingdom. A fierce conflict in 1253 between the archbishop of Embrun (Hautes-Alpes) and his city was settled by an arbitration which allowed the city to acquire land to widen roads and so on only if it would be clearly for the common good (*pro evidenti utilitate communi*) and for a payment allowed by a judge.[91] The dauphin's grant of liberties in 1309 to La Mure (Isère) gave the burgesses license to acquire land for walls and roads, erect a market hall, and do other things for the public good (*ad publicam utilitatem*), paying for it all by the assessment of worthy men.[92] These seem to be exceptional cases: the bulk of the charters suggest that the right of autonomous local communities to take land for the public or common good may have been taken for granted, just as was the right of a lord to take it for that purpose. References to the *utilitas* or *communis utilitas* of towns start in the twelfth century

89. *Elenchus*, vol. 2(1), nos. 93, 95.
90. Barckhausen, *Livre des coutumes*, no. 62.
91. Roman, "Les statuts."
92. Dussert, *Essai historique sur La Mure*, 479–86.

and seem to be most frequent in the south, but the phrase does not seem to be connected to any particular rights:[93] the general tenor of the charters suggests that it was simply a good way of referring to an obvious and general concern. As for actual cases of expropriation by towns, the fact that I found no examples from France before the late Middle Ages may also testify to the way that the whole thing was taken for granted — as well as to the need for more thorough searches than I have made.

Growth in the general activity and bureaucracy of royal government, along with better records, may explain the impression that royal expropriations started or multiplied from the late thirteenth century. Exclusive attention to royal rights may, however, be misleading. It is doubtful that they were part of what has (rather anachronistically) been called the king's "domaine eminent,"[94] and that this should be connected with ideas of feudal hierarchy. Though seizures by kings may have been particularly hard to resist, it was not only they who took property. Compensation may have been harder to get from kings, but, like other lords and local communities, they seem to have been supposed to pay it. By the sixteenth century, lawyers believed that a royal ordinance of 1304 had allowed churches to expropriate land they needed on their own initiative.[95] This, I suggest, derived from a misunderstanding of the ordinance, which seems to have granted exemptions from laws controlling and restricting grants of property to the church (*amortissement* or, in English common law, "mortmain") rather than giving a general right to expropriate.[96] Since churches were assumed to exist for the common good, land could be taken for their use, but it is not clear that they could take it without royal (or other secular) authorization.

93. See, e.g., *Elenchus*, vol. 2(1), index, under "*utilitas.*"
94. Leyte, *Domaine et domanialité*, 190–92.
95. Domat, *Les loix civiles*, 51; Cilleuls, *Origines*, 89 and n. 16; Mestre, *Un droit administrative*, 300.
96. *Ordonnances des roys de France*, 1:404, c. 12–14, 406–12; for the laws on *amortissement*, see ibid., 303–5, 322–26, 745–49.

All classes of landowner below the king and all categories of land appear to have been, in principle if not in practice, liable to expropriation. It was not apparently a "feudal" matter in the sense that lords were officially allowed to take land more easily from those who held fiefs from them; that allods were exempt; or that a greater right of expropriation from the unfree was explicitly and officially permitted or thought just. The compensation paid, or at least owed, to both owners and occupiers of the houses in Paris taken for Philip IV's palace suggests a different pattern of norms.[97] The origin of the norms that seem to have been accepted remains obscure, but I conclude provisionally that there is no reason to see expropriation for the common good, with compensation, as having originated in opposition to expropriation by lords in their own interest, with or without compensation.

In 1338, in answer to complaints from a wide area of the south, Philip VI agreed that he would not acquire property in areas where his petitioners had high justice, or *merum imperium*, except for fortifications needed (*necessaria vel utilia*) for the security of the kingdom. In such cases he would make recompense.[98] In 1358 the king's lieutenant in Gascony gave permission to consuls or syndics of local communities to demolish buildings for the common good (*pro bono publico*), fortification, and security of the communities, compensating their owners.[99] In 1407 the royal rights were stated more positively than before: for the good, protection, and defense of his people and the public good (*l'utilité de la chose publique*) of his kingdom, the king, like his predecessors, had the right and duty to take land, castles, ports, and other places that he considered necessary for the care and defense of his subjects and the security (*la seureté universelle*) of his kingdom, making due recompense.[100] In 1470 the king authorized the mayor and councillors

---

97. See n. 79, above. On later medieval expropriations by French kings (and lords), see Leyte, *Domaine et domanialité*, 189–94, 425–32.
98. *Ordonnances des roys de France*, 2:128, c. 33.
99. Isambert et al., *Recueil général*, vol. 5, no. 276, c. 15.
100. Cilleuls, *Origines*, 88.

(*échevins*) of Amiens, and their successors, to take land needed for the fortification of the town after consultation with the royal *bailli* or his subordinate. Reasonable compensation was to be made.[101] In 1510 an ordinance gave authority to royal officers, with the advice of mayors, *échevins*, and inhabitants of towns, to have houses demolished, with compensation, for the widening of streets and squares.[102] In 1547 another, issued at the request of the Estates and Parlement of Provence, allowed the owners of mills and all other contrivances (*tous autres engins*) to make watercourses, sluices, and the like over the land of others, with suitable payments. This particular order, however, was apparently considered not as authorizing expropriation but as creating servitudes (i.e., easements in English common law).[103]

From now on the taking of land for roads and other public works was quite often authorized by the royal council.[104] By the eighteenth century, while towns sometimes, at least in some areas, still acted on their own initiative, they often sought approval from the council, while urban public works, by now including town planning, were often organized by the local royal intendant. Compensation was sometimes assessed by experts or royal officials rather than by the local "good men" often referred to in medieval documents.[105] In the case of new roads, landowners could be compensated by letting them have the land of the old line of the road to replace what they had given up for the new.[106] The demolition of houses to stop the spread of fire was said not

---

101. *Ordonnances des roys de France*, 17:401.
102. Cilleuls, *Origines*, 89.
103. Morgues, *Statuts et coustumes*, 230–31, 233; Mestre, *Un droit administrative*, 263–64, 318–19.
104. Vignon, *Études historiques*, 1:18–21, 79–81; Cilleuls, *Origines*, 88–109; Dareste and Dareste, *La justice administrative*, 455–59, 587–89; Harouel, "L'expropriation," 53–67.
105. Harouel, *L'embellissement des villes*, 84–58, 263–69.
106. Petot, *Histoire de l'administration*, 56, 93–95.

to require compensation.[107] Until 1789, although local autonomy was increasingly restricted, it was not formally eliminated. J.-L. Mestre has shown how much expropriation was done in Provence with little or no reference to the central government.[108] Other *pays d'état* may have exercised similar authority. In Provence, as Mestre shows, the right to expropriate was enjoyed in the seventeenth century not only by towns and rural communities but by churches, lords, and individuals carrying out what could be represented as public works. Perhaps this was at least partly explained by what I have suggested was a misunderstanding of Philip IV's ordinance of 1304. In the eighteenth century, under the influence of Grotius, Provençal lawyers changed their views: local communities continued to be allowed to expropriate on their own initiative, by decision of their councils, but churches had to seek legal authorization.

The complexity of regional variations in government, of local jurisdictions, and of property rights made expropriation difficult and complicated, but that may have been largely the effect of the development of professional law, which multiplied and entrenched complexities, rather than of the survival of "feudal" rights as they had existed before the late Middle Ages.[109] It is difficult to imagine that land taken for public works in the Middle Ages would have been carefully detached from the fiefs to which it had once belonged and made into a new fief to be held from the king with all levels of justice, as happened when land was taken for the Canal du Languedoc in 1665.[110] Though medieval custom had generally considered castles, as works of defense, to be for the

---

107. La Mare, *Traité de la police*, 4:158–59.

108. Mestre, *Un droit administrative*, 297–332; Cilleuls, *Origines*, 109 nn. 17–18.

109. Petot, *Histoire de l'administration*, 285, 319; Cheyette, "La justice et le pouvoir royal."

110. Lalande, *Des canaux de navigation*, 115–18; Maistre, *Le canal des deux mers*, 64–72, 137–49.

common good, the Provençal professor of law who maintained that a vassal could be compelled to sell land needed for his lord's castle was clearly drawing on the academic law of fiefs rather than on medieval custom.[111]

Despite all the various royal ordinances referred to above, the assumption that expropriation was a matter for the sovereign government seems, in France, as elsewhere, to have become established as a result of increasing supervision by sovereign governments rather than of formal legislation. The Declarations of Rights issued in 1789 and 1793 were, on this subject, entirely unrevolutionary, allowing property to be taken for public necessity and for just and prior compensation.[112] Meanwhile, when the revolutionary government needed land for an arms factory in 1794, compensation was duly paid in advance.[113] The confiscation of church property was, of course, like the seizure of property from Protestants by Louis XIV and from the Jesuits when they were expelled in 1764, justified by the national interest, though the expulsion of the Jesuits was also justified by a long list of accusations against them.[114] The revolutionary expropriation of the church was, however, rather different from these earlier confiscations, insofar as it was rather more like the kind of expropriation for the sake of redistribution that I have excluded from my subject. Even more clearly over that boundary were the sequestrations of the property of émigrés in 1792 and of enemies of the republic in 1794.[115]

---

111. Mestre, *Un droit administrative*, 307.

112. Roberts and Hardman, *French Revolution Documents*, 1:68, 173 (c. 17); 2:140–41 (cc. 16, 19).

113. Gross, *Fair Shares*, 95.

114. Roberts and Hardman, *French Revolutionary Documents*, 1:186, 383–86; McManners, *Church and Society*, 2:553–60; *Arrest de la cour de parlement . . . 6 août 1762*.

115. Leroy, *Histoire des idées sociales*, 1:266–70.

3.5 GERMANY

Germany here is taken, as I explained at the beginning of the chapter, to cover, more or less, the area of the medieval kingdom, including examples from what are now the Netherlands, Belgium, Austria, and France (Strasbourg). However it is defined, it presents slightly different problems about the history of expropriation from those of France and England. The way that historians of those two countries have traced the development of governmental control, respectively by the royal council and by parliament, makes the postmedieval history relatively easy to trace, at least in outline. This sort of teleology is inhibited by the fragmentation of authority in Germany from the later Middle Ages to 1870, which makes it more difficult, especially for someone unfamiliar with the secondary literature and sources of the period. On the other hand, though some German legal and urban historians, like many concerned with France and England, have more or less ignored expropriation before the eighteenth or nineteenth century,[116] not all, to my profit, have done so. Some of them start from the discouraging premise that expropriation has always been essentially the prerogative of sovereign governments and was unknown to earlier German law,[117] and nearly all concentrate on treatises and formal legislation rather than practice. My search of an admittedly restricted bibliography has nevertheless produced enough to sug-

---

116. E.g., in more recent works, to judge from their indexes: Conrad, *Deutsche Rechtsgeschichte*; Kroeschell, *Deutsche Rechtsgeschichte* [to 1650]; Jeserich et al., *Deutsche Verwaltungsgeschichte*; Eisenhardt, *Deutsche Rechtsgeschichte*; Stolleis, *Geschichte des öffentlichen Rechts in Deutschland*. On Austria see Baltl and Rocher, *Österreichische Rechtsgeschichte*.

117. Meyer, *Das Recht der Expropriation*, 70–76, seems to have been often followed, as late, e.g., as 1964 (Erler and Kaufmann, *Handwörterbuch zur deutschen Rechtsgeschichte*, 1:941–44), though Gierke apparently doubted Meyer's view on the absence from early German law: see Gierke, *Deutsches Privatrecht*, 2:466 n.

gest that both norms and practice may have been not very different from what I have argued they were in the countries I have so far considered.

Hans Planitz provided the earliest example of expropriation by a town north of the Alps that I have found. In his earlier work he saw expropriation in the common interest as a development of the fourteenth century, presumably partly because he had accepted the traditional view that it was unknown to early German law.[118] In *Die deutsche Stadt im Mittelalter*, published in 1954, however, he cited several occasions in the thirteenth century when German towns took land for their fortifications in exchange either for money or for other land.[119] The earliest of these came from 1239, when the town of Strasbourg gave an island to one of its citizens in exchange for one he owned that they needed for their wall and ditch.[120] As is often the case elsewhere at this period, it is not entirely clear how far all the cases involved compulsion rather than agreement, but when in 1273 the whole town of Trier compensated the Templars for land already taken for the town walls and ditch for the common good of the citizens (*pro communi utilitate civium*), it looks very like a classic expropriation.[121] As elsewhere, it seems probable that the evidence of these cases and others later is more the product of new record keeping than of entirely new practices and ideas about the common good.

Despite occasional royal commands, permissions, and prohibitions about building fortifications, it does not seem that towns, or indeed villages, in practice needed permission to build their own fortifications or take land for them here any more than I

---

118. Planitz, *Grundzüge des deutschen Privatrechts*, 72, and *Germanische Rechtsgeschichte*, 205.

119. Planitz, *Die deutsche Stadt*, 321–22, though his Cologne cases seem not to be quite expropriations, and I have not been able to see his sources for Kiel or Freiburg im Breisgau.

120. Wiegand, *Urkundenbuch der Stadt Strassburg*, vol. 1, no. 261.

121. Rudolph, *Kurtrierische Städte*, vol. 1: *Trier*, 288.

have suggested they did in the other countries I survey. Getting a formal authorization and keeping a record of it could be useful without being essential.[122] Most charters issued to German (including Austrian) towns before the mid-thirteenth century, like those issued to French towns, are full of rules about judicial procedures and penalties and refer only in passing, if at all, to town walls.[123] Some such references suggest particular circumstances. In 1159, for instance, the archbishop of Magdeburg exempted the inhabitants of a new settlement from work on fortifications (*burgwere*) unless they needed to build their own. In 1220 the lord of Trazegnies (Hainaut, Belgium) assumed that the town *scabini* were responsible for their walls, though with the help of wood provided by his forester.[124] In 1229 the duke of Lotharingia issued a charter to Maastricht in which, since the common good was to be preferred to the private (*quoniam communis utilitas private preferenda est*), he authorized the town to build walls for the common good (*ob communem utilitatem*), as all the better towns nearby had them. The following year the bishop of Utrecht told the people of Zwolle (Overijssel, Netherlands) that they could make their villa an *oppidum* and fortify it.[125] None of these documents mentioned how the necessary land was to be acquired. That was, I deduce, for the local communities to arrange for the common good. Cornelius van Bynkershoek, writing in the eighteenth century, illustrated his arguments about public law with cases from the Netherlands since the late fourteenth century as well as from the texts of Roman law. He deduced from charters granted by counts, emperors, or kings that towns needed permission from above to

---

122. Churches getting permission: e.g., *Diplomata Regum et Imperatorum*, vol. 1: Otto I, no. 27; *Constitutiones et Acta Publica*, vol. 2, no. 306; *Elenchus*, vol. 3 (pt. 1), nos. 72, 93.

123. See, e.g., *Elenchus*, 1:152, 156, 174, 176; vol. 3 (pt. 1), nos. 46, 54, 57, 66, 67, 69, 75, 89.

124. Ibid., 1:126–27, 376–77 (cc. 8–9).

125. Ibid., 1:457–58.

build walls or public buildings like courthouses, whether or not that involved taking land. Obtaining charters may, however, have been more precautionary than essential in the earlier cases he cites, as when Amsterdam and Leiden received charters in 1386 from Albert of Bavaria, count of Holland, to build new walls and acquire land for them. The statutes of both towns allowed their councils to take land as necessary.[126]

Information from outside towns is harder to come by, except in relation to the law about mines (*Bergrecht*) and dykes (*Deichrecht*), which German historians see as involving special kinds of expropriation.[127] I shall not discuss mines, first, because the taking of land for them does not seem to fall under the usual norms about the common good. Second, it is not clear whether the various rules inferred from earlier medieval references involved expropriation. When professional law developed in the later Middle Ages and after, property rights in Germany became divided so that the landowner's property was restricted to the surface. As a result, though landowners had to allow prospecting and access, no question of actual expropriation seems to have arisen.[128] The taking of land for dykes, on the other hand, whether in the sense of banks constructed to hold back water or in that of ditches or artificial watercourses, falls within my deliberately restricted subject and indeed provides the only medieval nonurban references I have found for what was then the Kingdom of Germany.[129] Not that I have many of them: local regulations about dyke building and repairing in Friesland seem often to have assumed that the dykes were already there. Some are mentioned as under the control of local communities and were presumably, in effect, their collective property, while some communities seem to have been able to assign land to them as they saw fit within the territories

---

126. Bynkershoek, *Quaestionum Juris Publici Libri Duo*, 213–17.
127. See, e.g. Neusser, "Enteignung," 942.
128. Wegener, "Bergrecht"; Arndt, "Bergbau."
129. In general: Anschütz, "Deichwesen."

over which they had authority.[130] There may be a hint at expropriation in the permission given in 1251 by William, count of Holland (and also king of the Romans), to an abbess in Holland to embank (*aggerandum*) her new land, since he also ordered that justice should be done to anyone who could show that they were damaged.[131] The order issued in 1288 to Utrecht by a later count to make a ditch or aqueduct on land that had been adjudged to the city, after the city had paid money adjudged to the former owners of the land, is also suggestive, if no more.[132] In 1376, at the other end of the empire, the duke of Austria had an enquiry made about a watercourse (*graben*) that the local community of the Tullner field outside Vienna had already made (*der leut gemeinlich auf dem Tulner veld gemachet*). He ordered that anyone, noble or nonnoble, rich or poor, who made use of the watercourse should contribute to its maintenance. His intervention may have been prompted by complaints from people who alleged that their land had been taken without compensation: if it had been, he said, they were to be compensated.[133] Few as they are, these cases suggest that expropriations needed for waterworks may at least sometimes have been managed by local communities, with or without the help or intervention of their immediate lords, more or less as a matter of course and probably with some sort of compensation.

From the sixteenth century, towns and dyke communities, no doubt like other units of local government, came under closer control by the governments of the principalities in which they lay, just as those in France and England came respectively under royal or parliamentary control.[134] How this affected the practice of expropriation has been very little discussed in the legal histories I

---

130. Richthoven, *Friesische Rechtsquellen*.
131. Van den Bergh, *Oorkondenboek van Holland en Zeeland*, vol. 1, no. 534.
132. Ibid., vol. 2, no. 640.
133. Loersch and Schroeder, *Urkunden zur Geschichte des deutschen Privatrechtes*, no. 197.
134. Haase, "Die mittelalterliche Stadt als Festung," 1:384.

have seen. Grotius did not illustrate his remarks about expropriation in *De Iure Belli ac Pacis* with examples, but his introduction to Dutch law refers to the construction and repair of dykes and to town improvements as done by the authority of local officials. Since this comes in a section discussing how property rights could be lost, it looks as if Grotius thought the officials could take land as well as materials from it. Either way, just compensation must be made.[135] Bynkershoek's emphasis on the need for authorization is more justified for this period than for the later Middle Ages, even if it reflected his understanding of Roman law as well as the actual cases from the Netherlands that he cites. Most of his sixteenth- and seventeenth-century examples illustrate the problems of fortification in rebellions and wars, but not all. In 1574 William of Orange ordered that private houses and other private and public property should be taken, with compensation, not only to build but to beautify the new academy that was being founded in Leiden and to allow space for the students' recreation — an extension of the concept of the common good of which Bynkershoek disapproved.[136] In other Dutch cases that he cited, permission was given by the estates of the province concerned. In 1732 the Estates of Zeeland even took property from the heir of William III of Orange, who refused the offered compensation. The case was undecided when Bynkershoek was writing.

Samuel von Pufendorf, writing a few decades after Grotius, illustrated his discussion of expropriation for the needs of the state (*reipublicae necessitas*) or common good (*propter salutem publicam*) chiefly from ancient history, but his reference to urban fortifications may reflect conditions in seventeenth-century Germany.[137] During the Thirty Years War, according to an essay of 1918 clearly based on Prussian state archives, the Great Elector,

---

135. Grotius, *Inleidinge*, 151–52 (II.32.7).
136. Bynkershoek, *Quaestionum Juris Publici Libri Duo*, 213–23; [Lulius], *Rechtsgeleerde Observatien*, 72–74.
137. Pufendorf, *De Iure Naturae*, 1:875–76 (VIII.5.7).

Frederick William, took land for the fortification of Berlin, with at least partial though delayed compensation and after considerable discussion in the Landtag.[138]

There must have been many cases that I have missed, while others that I have mentioned, like those from Bynkershoek, need further substantiation. Many have been missed by those legal historians who, even if they are interested in expropriation, tend to rely on the evidence of formal legislation. The absence of legislation need not imply that expropriation was not going on, just as its appearance need not imply innovation: law codes and other legislation may reflect what was accepted and had already been happening in practice. The Bavarian *Landrecht* of 1616 refers to the taking of land for roads, and the *Codex Maximilianus* of 1756 says that no one could be compelled to sell property against their will unless the government (*die Landes- und Polizei-Ordnung*) needed it for the common good (*um des gemeinen Besten*).[139] In the late eighteenth century it was accepted in Bavaria that the ruler (*Landesherr*) had the right to take land for highways that were needed for the common good (*des allgemeinen Bessten*) and that compensation should be made for it. Road building was administered by government inspectors, but there were uncertainties about liabilities and procedures that were addressed in ordinances of 1815 and 1837. The demolition of houses to prevent the spread of fire was mentioned in 1839 among reasons for expropriation that had been accepted before these clarifications.[140] By this time the Prussian law code of 1794 had set the pattern of later codes. Like the Bavarian code of 1756 — and like the French and American declarations, though, unsurprisingly, with less revolutionary flourish than either of them — it ruled that the state could compel

---

138. Holtz, "Krieg und Enteignung."

139. *Landrecht* (1616), 595 (3.13.3); Danzer, *Bayerische Landrecht*, 223 (4.3.2).

140. Mayr, *Sammlung der Churpfalz-Baierischen . . . Landes-Verordnungen*, 5:117 (4.20.18); Samhaber, *Das k. bayerische Gesetz*, 1837, 15–21.

anyone to sell property (*Sache*) only when it was needed for the common good (*zum Besten des gemeinen Wesens*). The state was obliged to compensate anyone who gave up rights or privileges for the community. One example given was the taking of land for roads, with compensation.[141]

The evidence I have found, largely through serendipity, is much too slight and scattered to justify conclusions about all the German principalities and cities. Perhaps, however, it may be just enough, when taken alongside that for other countries, to support the hypothesis that expropriation for the common good, generally with compensation, was probably accepted and practiced in Germany and the Netherlands, and probably by decisions taken locally according to custom, long before the growth either of the ideas of absolutism or of state power in practice with which some historians have associated it.

3.6 SPAIN

The sources on Spain for my account of expropriation are not even derived from the serendipity that produced my German material. Though friends interested in medieval Spain have helped me, most of my examples come from references given by F. L. Pacheco Caballero in an essay published in 2000 and from Francisco de Cárdenas's book of 1873 on the history of Spanish property that Pacheco cited.[142]

In 1126 Alfonso VII of Castile and León issued a charter in which he confessed that during the troubles under his mother, Queen Urraca, he had taken from the abbey of Sahagún both treasure and land (*villas ceterasque possessiones*) to give to his soldiers. He said that he had done it because he had been pressed by many needs and driven by the irresponsibility of youth (*multis necces-*

---

141. *Allgemeines Landrecht für die Preussischen Staate*, vol. 1(1), 12–13 (Einleitung, 73–74), vol. 2(2), 223.
142. Pacheco Caballero, "La recepción hispánica"; Cárdenas, *Ensayo*.

sitatibus coangustatus et levi adolescentie sensu agitatus).[143] Since then he had, it seems, had second thoughts, no doubt fostered by the monks. Pacheco, following the argument of J.-L. Mestre about France, casts some doubt on the public good as justification for a lord (and presumably therefore also a king) to take land before the revival of Roman law, but I have already argued that the evidence for Mestre's thesis is unconvincing. There is at least some evidence that the public good, and especially the defense of a kingdom, was used in other countries well before this time, however controversially or disingenuously, to justify the taking of land even from churches. Alfonso's charter says that his taking of Sahagún's property had been against old custom: perhaps Castilian custom had not hitherto recognized the justification but, even if churches like Sahagún found the justification hard to accept, it could perhaps, on the analogy of other countries, have been thought valid by kings and their counselors and maybe by the laity in general. Perhaps it was not, and the custom of Castile, and perhaps other Spanish kingdoms, did not yet allow land to be taken for the common good of the kingdom. The evidence of the collective activity of local communities and of their collective rights in land (including cultivated land), as early as the tenth century nevertheless suggests at least the possibility that some of them may have assumed that they could take land from their members when it was needed for their common purposes.[144]

A charter of 1179 suggests that the norm was then accepted by at least one king and some of his counselors, though still contested by some of the clergy. It records the restoration by Ferdinand II of León to the Hospital of St. John of property that he had taken, wrongly and on bad advice, for the good and enrichment (or enlargement) of his kingdom (*ad utilitatem et nostri regni incrementum*).[145] He had apparently settled people on the land

---

143. Mínguez Fernández, *Colección diplomática de Sahagún*, 4, no. 1226.
144. See chapter 2.5.
145. Gonzales, *Regesta de Fernando II*, no. 37.

he had taken. The *fueros*, or customs, of Cuenca and Plasencia (both in Castile), and of Teruel (just over the border in Aragon), were all probably compiled between the late twelfth century and the mid-thirteenth. All seem concerned to control and protect building materials.[146] In the Cuenca *fuero* and the Latin version of that of Teruel the materials were explicitly those for building walls — presumably the town defenses. In Plasencia and in the Spanish version of the Teruel *fuero*, all quarried stone, gypsum, millstones, roofing materials, and permanent springs or wells (Plasencia: *todos pedreras et gesseras et moleras et tegeres et otrossi fuentes perenales*) were to be common property. Anyone who had any of them on his land should sell them to the community for double their value.

The great law book *Siete Partidas*, compiled for Alfonso X in the 1260s, is full of influences from the academic study of Roman law, but it also presumably reflects Castilian practice and perhaps fairly well-established Castilian norms. The emperor (or king) can take anyone's property, but he can do it only by law, either with the consent of the owner or as punishment. If he does it out of need for the common good of the country (*pro communal dela tierra*), he is bound by law to give in exchange something worth as much or more in the view of good men (*a bien vista de omes buenos*).[147] Although I have happened on no examples from Catalonia or Aragon (apart from the Teruel *fuero*) before the late thirteenth century, those who know the field better might find some. In the meantime I see no reason why either area should have been very different from Castile or indeed from France, Italy, and other countries where expropriation, with compensation, was

---

146. Ureña y Smenjaud, *Fuero de Cuenca*, 814 (c. 43:4); Ramírez Vaquero, *Fuero de Plasencia*, 1:152 (c. 630), 161 (c. 686). Pacheco Caballero, "La recepción hispánica," 166 n. 10 has the text of part of these: Gorosch, *Fuero de Teruel*, 228 (c. 325); Caruana Gomez de Barreda, *Fuero latino de Teruel*, 428 (c. 540).

147. López, *Siete partidas*, vol. 2, fols. 3v–4r (II.1.2).

apparently taken for granted — at least by the laity. That seems to have been the case in 1283, when the royal court at Barcelona ordered that a bridge be built over the river Llobregat *ad rocham*, but added that anyone whom it might damage should be compensated.[148] Tomas Mieres, writing in the fifteenth century about royal rights of expropriation, perhaps with further information about the case, saw it as having involved the taking of property.[149] Kings of Aragon in the thirteenth and fourteenth centuries apparently tried on several occasions to make the owners of salt mines sell them to the crown but with only temporary success. In 1325, if not on other occasions when the owners succeeded in getting their mines back, they had to repay what the king had given for what he had taken.[150] In 1564, when Philip II finally took over all the salt mines, his ordinance says that it was done for the public good (*que tanto importa al bien y beneficio publico*) and was compensated by a just price (*recopensa justa*).[151]

The concentration of the *Siete Partidas* on royal rights was presumably determined, as were the discussions of Italian lawyers, by starting from the Roman law texts,[152] so that it need not imply that in Spain expropriation was in practice reserved to kings. The *fueros* already mentioned suggest that it was not, and so does the building of castles in late medieval and sixteenth-century Castile. My restricted searches have not shown whether the demolitions of unlicensed castles ordered by kings of Castile involved the taking of the land on which the condemned castles stood, so as to

---

148. *Cortes de Aragon*, vol. 1 (1), 152 (c. 47). I have not identified the *rocha*: neither it nor the bridge is mentioned in Garcia Espuche et al., "Barcelona."

149. Pacheco, "La recepción hispánica," 167 n., 172–73.

150. Cárdenas, *Ensayo*, 222–29; Parral y Cristóbal, *Fueros y observancias*, fol. 10v. The properties restored in 1283 (ibid., fol. 8v, and Zurita, *Anales*, 2:140) are not there specified as salt mines, and their taking may anyway not have been justified by the public good.

151. *Recopilacion de las leyes*, vol. 3, fols. 64r–65r (IX.19).

152. See chapter 4.2.

count as expropriation.[153] In the fifteenth century, when lords had houses demolished to make way for castles and town walls, the demolitions presumably involved the taking of the land on which the houses had stood. The lords concerned were considered to owe compensation, even though they did not always pay it or pay it at once.[154] Although those who claimed compensation could appeal to royal courts for it, that does not seem to imply that the actual expropriation had needed royal permission. The expulsion of the Jews in 1492 and the taking of their property was presented, as in other countries, as done for the service of God and the general good of the native subjects of the Spanish kingdoms (*bien e provecho comun de nuestros reynos e de nuestros subditos e naturales dellos*).[155]

From the late sixteenth century on, when it seems to have gradually come to be assumed in all the areas I have studied that the right to expropriate was reserved to sovereign governments, the few Spanish cases I have happened on were indeed ordered by the royal government. The making of the Plaza Mayor in Madrid and the straightening of streets nearby between 1582 and 1620 involved the demolition of houses, probably with the taking of the land on which they stood. The project was authorized by the king, though the town government was responsible for compensation, which it paid in various ways, including exchanges of land.[156] In 1788, when houses in some of the streets and alleys of Madrid were thought to need alteration in order to improve the appearance of the town, those who failed to do the required work on their properties within a year would have them sold by public auction.[157]

---

153. Cárdenas, *Ensayo*, 118–19; *Cortes de Leon*, 1:335 (cc. 22–23), 348 (c. 41); Cooper, *Castillos señoriales*, 83–84.
154. Cooper, *Castillos señoriales*, 227, 469, 603–4, 998–99, 1499.
155. León Tello, *Judios de Toledo*, 1:543.
156. Escobar, *Plaza Mayor*, 89–126, 152–70.
157. *Novisima Recopilacion*, 2:154 (III.19.7), quoted in Pacheco Caballero, "La recepción hispánica", 172 n. 27.

Eighteenth-century plans for agrarian improvement in Spain, as in England, involved expropriations that their official promoters thought would be for the common good. Whereas in England, however, enclosures were promoted by landowners and merely authorized by parliament, the Spanish schemes came from the central government and its advisers, and the profits from their sale went to the crown.[158] The expulsion of the Jesuits in 1767 was presented as done for the tranquility and justice of the king's people and other urgent, just, and necessary reasons.[159] The profits from such of their property as was auctioned went to the government. Confiscations of religious and charitable property in 1798 were treated the same way.[160]

The first written Spanish constitution, passed in 1812, did no more than reflect traditional norms when it forbade the king to take the property of any individual or corporation except in case of necessity and for the common good (*para un objeto de conocida utilidad común*) and with compensation assessed by good men (*a bien vista de hombres buenos*).[161]

3.7 THE ENGLISH COLONIES IN AMERICA

English colonists in North America sometimes seized land from the native inhabitants or bought it for unduly small prices, but from the late seventeenth century to the end of the eighteenth it was generally agreed that the Indians had genuine rights of property which ought not to be totally ignored.[162] By the late eighteenth century, opinion was shifting. By 1823 a principle was accepted, as Chief Justice Marshall put it, "that the Indian inhabitants [were] to be considered merely as occupants, to be protected,

---

158. Herr, *Rural Change*, 19–20.
159. *Novísima Recopilacion*, 1:180–83 (I.26.3); Herr, *Rural Change*, 44–45.
160. *Novísima Recopilacion*, 1:51–52 (I.5.22); Herr, *Rural Change*, 93–94.
161. *Constitutiones y leyes fundamentales*, 134 (arts. 172, §10, 173).
162. Banner, *How the Indians Lost Their Land*, 10–90.

indeed, while in peace, in the possession of their lands, but to be deemed incapable of transferring the absolute title to others."[163] Either way, norms or rules about expropriation and compensation do not seem to have applied to Indian land, presumably because it was more or less outside the frontier of settlement and its holders did not belong to the community to whose common good European property was supposed to be subject.

Practice within the English colonies seems to have more or less followed that in England. As in early modern England, there are not many explicit references to the common good, but something of the sort seems to be implied as justifying expropriation. American legal historians seem to have accepted that colonial governments from the start, or very soon after, took land from colonists for public purposes. They have, however, disagreed about the need for compensation. It has been suggested that "the principle that the state should compensate individuals for property taken for public use was not widely established in America at the time of the Revolution."[164] This argument seems to have relied chiefly on the absence or late date of legislation about highways in some colonies and on two assumptions that may not be justified. The first is that only "states" (i.e., sovereign governments) could expropriate, and the second, that legislation and consistent judicial decisions were necessary to make an "inviolable rule."[165] Enough examples of the payment of compensation before the Revolution have, however, been cited to make the argument that it was not generally thought to be due less than convincing.[166] It is made even less so when the American evidence is seen against the back-

---

163. Wheaton, *Reports*, 8:543–605 (*Johnson v. M'Intosh*), quote at 591.

164. Horwitz, *Transformation*, 63 (in both 1977 and 1992 editions).

165. Ibid.; Treanor, "Origins," and (for the "inviolable rule") "Original Understanding," 788 n.; Hart, "Expropriation in America before 1776"; Sackman, *Nichols' The Law*, 1:76–86.

166. Especially by Ely, "'That Due Satisfaction Be Made,'" to which my argument and evidence owe much; Stoebuck, "General Theory," 580–82.

ground of centuries in which the need for compensation had been taken for granted in Europe, including England, though with very little legislation or judicial statement of rules.

Attention has focused especially on roads. In 1632 it was ordered in Virginia that highways should be laid out by agreement of the governor and council, the commissioners of monthly courts, or parishioners, and it was resolved not to pay for any land taken.[167] Eleven years later Massachusetts ordered that "reasonable satisfaction" should be made for damage to anyone's "improved ground," according to valuations made by the town representatives who were to lay out the roads.[168] Thereafter there seems to be more evidence of payment for land taken for roads in the northern than the southern colonies, which has been explained by differences in their social, political, and economic structures.[169] Since southern colonies paid for land that they took for public buildings of various sorts, the lack of legislation about compensation for what was taken for roads may say more about the different need for roads, their layout, and use than about ideas on expropriation and compensation, as such.[170] The abundance of land allowed colonists to adopt different attitudes to it from those prevailing in Europe, and they may well have adapted their ideas in slightly different ways according to local circumstances. The way land was allocated varied. Unoccupied or unenclosed land, for instance, could in some areas and at some times be taken without compensation, though not necessarily without argument.[171] Compensation was sometimes paid, including in Virginia, for materials taken for road repairs,

---

167. Hening, *Statutes of Virginia*, 1:199; though cf. compensation ordered later: ibid., 6:213, §3.
168. Cushing, *Laws and Liberties of Massachusetts*, 1:25.
169. Hart, "Taking and Compensation" and "Expropriation in America before 1776."
170. Ely, "'That Due Satisfaction Be Made,'" with references.
171. Hart, "Expropriation in America before 1776"; Treanor, "Origins"; Lincoln et al., *Colonial Laws of New York*, 2:63–64, and later laws.

which it was not in England.[172] In early nineteenth-century Massachusetts, and perhaps elsewhere and at other times, roads could be treated as easements, so that the landowner was compensated without losing title.[173]

As in England, a good deal of the early legislation about roads was concerned more with getting surveyors and parishioners to fulfill their obligations of repair and maintenance than with the kind of widening or straightening of roads that might call for compensation.[174] The early legislation suggests that English colonists started, unsurprisingly, from English practice: parishes appointed surveyors to make their neighbors do the work or pay for it. When compensation was needed (whether land was taken for roads or other purposes), it seems quite often, if not generally, to have been assessed by two or three, or twelve, sworn men of the neighborhood, supervised by justices of the peace, to whom appeal might be allowed.[175] The New York act for the fortification of Schenectady evokes even older European precedents from a time when it had been assumed that towns should be fortified for the good of their inhabitants, but that land taken for walls would be paid for.[176] The JPs, officers, and captains who were to organize the work at Schenectady and share out expenses and labor among the freeholders of the town were to "endeavour in a Friendly and Amicable manner" to purchase the land needed. If the owners

---

172. Ely, "'That Due Satisfaction Be Made,'" 11.

173. William Nelson, *Americanization*, 236–37.

174. See, e.g., Hening, *Statutes of Virginia*, 1:436, 2:103; Shurtleff, *Records of New Plymouth*, 1:31, 39, 98, 117, 141; Lincoln, *Colonial Laws of New York*, 1:225–26, 471–72, 532–38, 794–95; Bush, *Laws of New Jersey*, 2:197.

175. Cushing, *Laws and Liberties of Massachusetts*, 1:25; *Acts and Resolves of Massachusetts*, 1:136–37; Hoadly, *Public Records of Connecticut*, 314–15; Hening, *Statutes of Virginia*, 6:55–56, 60, 9:315; Lincoln, *Colonial Laws of New York*, 1:471–72; 2:63–64, 70, 659–65, 736–41; 3:1074, 418–24, 474–80; *Archives of Maryland*, 64:397; Ely, "'That Due Satisfaction Be Made,'" 9.

176. See chapter 2.4 and earlier sections of this chapter.

would not agree, then twelve good and lawful men were to be sworn in to value it.[177]

Provision for compensation may have first appeared in the statutes of any colony because the need to take improved land was new there, or because someone objected to the taking of his land, rather than because the idea of either taking land or paying for what was taken was new or controversial. In 1692 the JPs and selectmen of Boston were authorized to lay out, straighten, and widen streets and passages, with compensation assessed by a jury. A year later a Massachusetts statute made committees of local freemen responsible for assessing the need for new roads, with possible appeal to quarter sessions about compensation.[178] This has been cited as evidence that Massachusetts alone "seems rigidly to have followed the principle for just compensation in road building"[179] but, whether or not Massachusetts in practice stuck rigidly to the rules laid down, Connecticut passed a statute in 1699 which followed that of Massachusetts almost word for word. Perhaps it simply copied a good model for stating a generally accepted norm. Given the difference from European circumstances, the variations between colonies, and the changes that took place in each, it seems possible that practice varied rather more than the legislation suggests. It is tempting to wonder whether towns in New England that made their own allocations of land may even have taken bits back without reference to colonial governors or assemblies.[180] Later on, mills came to pose problems that were solved in different ways.

By the eighteenth century, if not before, it seems to have been accepted in the American colonies, as in Europe, that expropriation needed authorization by central government, with colonial

---

177. Lincoln, *Colonial Laws of New York*, 3:1073–75.
178. *Acts and Resolves of Massachusetts*, 1:42–43, 136–37.
179. Horwitz, *Transformation*, 63.
180. Allen, *In English Ways*, 202–23; Mensch, "Colonial Origins"; Ely, "'That Due Satisfaction Be Made.'"

legislatures or governors filling that role here. This could have owed something to American respect for Blackstone, but it need not have, since his remarks merely reflected current English practice. Nor need it have been inspired by the reading of Vattel or other writers on natural law. Although Americans seem to have been much more given to reading foreign works on political theory than were English lawyers, their reading does not as yet seem to have affected practice — unsurprisingly, since the works they read did not seriously disagree with what was being done.[181] Although the natural law treatises often by now used the expression "eminent domain" and historians of American law tend to use it when writing about expropriation in the eighteenth century and earlier,[182] that is slightly misleading. The phrase does not seem to occur in the sources that the historians cite from before the Revolution and suggests an intellectual context that may not be appropriate to those dealing with expropriations in practice at that time. The first examples I have found of its use in America are in two cases, argued in South Carolina and Pennsylvania, in 1796.[183]

By that time successive state constitutions and bills of rights and then the federal bill, in what became the Fifth Amendment, had laid down an explicit right to compensation — which may be why historians have sometimes assumed that compulsory compensation was new and progressive.[184] Past practice and the apparent lack of argument about the compensation required by the Fifth Amendment suggests that it was not, though, of course, it may not always have been paid, or paid adequately. Property confiscated from loyalists in the War of Independence was not

---

181. Grant, "'Higher Law' Background"; Mayer, *Constitutional Thought of Thomas Jefferson*, 77–80; Franklin, *Writings*, "Queries and Remarks," 59; McDonald, *Novus Ordo Seclorum*, 3–23, 37, 58–94. See chapter 4.3.

182. Even, on occasion, in connection with the taking of nonlanded property: see William Nelson, *Americanization*, index, under "eminent domain."

183. See chapter 4.3, at nn. 78–80.

184. Cogan, *Complete Bill of Rights*, 361–74.

compensated from the American side, since they were considered to be enemies whose property could be taken under international law.[185] As the newly independent states began to embark on ambitious schemes of town planning, the making of canals, and so on, they needed to exercise the right of what was coming to be called eminent domain more often. The result was an increase in litigation and in developments in the law. That, however, largely took place after the period with which I have been concerned.

3.8 CONCLUSION

Patchy and partial as it is, the evidence presented in this chapter is, I believe, sufficient to show that from the twelfth century to the beginning of the nineteenth there was a general acceptance in a fairly large area of western Europe that land could be taken from individuals for what was perceived or presented as the common good, provided that compensation was made. The common good was taken to be that of political communities of some kind. At first these were understood as both kingdoms and lesser, local communities within them, but from the end of the Middle Ages they came gradually to be assumed to be those that were under governments that claimed to be in some sense sovereign, so that expropriation came to need authorization by their sovereign authorities.[186]

The impression I have received from most of the material surveyed in this chapter is that the principle of expropriation for what was taken to be the public good was so much taken for granted that most of the disputes about individual cases were about the amount of compensation. The work of Mestre on the early modern lawyers of Provence led me to wonder if that was an illusion derived from not having found secondary works on the records

---

185. Ford et al., *Journals of the Continental Congress*, 5:605–6; Kutler, *Dictionary of American History*, 2:346–47.

186. See chapter 5.

of courts and the papers of lawyers in other areas and periods.[187] From the time, around the twelfth and thirteenth centuries, when professional lawyers began to dominate higher courts, influence the procedures of government, and advise such landowners as could afford to pay them, they may well have challenged or promoted the rights of expropriation as well as the obligation to compensate the expropriated. More work on the subject is obviously needed.

---

187. See n. 103 above.

CHAPTER 4

Justifications and Discussions

4.1 THE PROBLEM

As I have argued, using the evidence I have cited, the justice of expropriation for the public good seems to have been largely taken for granted. That being so, the rarity of formal discussions of the principle may be hardly surprising. Individual expropriations were indeed often justified by the stated or implied reason that they were made for the common or public good. This, however, begs the question of the nature of property rights in land and of the apparently assumed priority over them of the good of the community, however defined. It also begs the question of the authority of the person or persons who ordered the expropriation. If it was done by a king or other supposedly independent ruler, his right may seem obvious, but the nature of the ruler's authority over the property of his subjects is generally left unclear: did the ruler act as representative of the community for its common good, or as the holder of a superior property right, as implied by theories of a feudal hierarchy of property? Expropriations by lesser authorities or communities raise further questions. So far as I have discovered, the first argument basing the right of expropriation firmly on the origin and nature of property rights seems to have been made in the seventeenth century by Hugo Grotius. Thereafter, influential as his work was, the connection between his arguments about expropriation and about wider matters of politics seems to have been largely ignored:[1] those who write about political thought tend to ignore expropriation while those who write about expropriation tend to ignore its implications for other rights.

4.2 BEFORE GROTIUS

The first approach to a discussion of the right of expropriation that I have found was made by the students of Roman law in twelfth-century Italy. It is reflected in an anecdote apparently first recorded in writing in an addition made to Otto Morena's chronicle about 1220.[2] The story is that Frederick Barbarossa asked Martinus and Bulgarus, two of the lawyers he consulted at Roncaglia in 1158, whether by law (or by right) he was lord of the world (*de iure esset dominus mundi*). Martinus said he was, but Bulgarus maintained that he was not *dominus quantum proprietatem*, that is, he did not have a property right in his subjects' property. In the story, Frederick thereupon gave his horse to Martinus, but most of the scholars of Roman law in the thirteenth and fourteenth centuries more or less agreed with Bulgarus. That did not mean that they thought the emperor or prince had no authority at all over his subjects' property, but that his authority extended only to protection and jurisdiction.[3] He was not thereby prevented from ever taking their property. He could do so, and there was some argument whether he needed a cause or reason for doing so, which presumably meant that he should or might say what the reason was. General opinion seems to have leaned toward the desirability of a just cause, whether stated or not. That qualification was sometimes supplemented or replaced by an explicit requirement that

---

1. This is further discussed in chapter 5.3.
2. Pennington, *Prince and the Law*, 15–30, discusses versions of the story and its implications.
3. Woolf, *Bartolus*, 23–25 nn., 46 n., quoting Bartolus, *Opera*, 1:9–10, 553; 7:112, with full references.

the property should be taken for the common or public good.[4] Since discussion started from Roman law texts dealing with the authority of the emperor, it is not surprising that nearly all of it was about expropriation by the prince or emperor.

Bartolus of Sassoferrato (d. 1357) was the first jurist I have found who extended the argument from the emperor, whose powers in Italy were by then rather theoretical, to independent cities. Bartolus reckoned that, whether they were free de jure (i.e., by imperial grant) or de facto, cities that recognized no superior had the same jurisdiction as the emperor or prince. They could therefore take the property of one of their subjects, though Bartolus implies this only by saying that they could not do it without cause. What he says elsewhere about the common good (*contra ius vel utilitatem publicam; ob publicam utilitatem*) suggests that he assumes that it was, or ought to be, what justified expropriation, just as it justified other acts of government.[5] As Cortese comments, medieval doctrine connected law and the public good (*causa legis, utilitas publica*) in many ways.[6] Bartolus's interest in making Roman law fit his own society worked for expropriation as it had gone on in Italian cities since at least the twelfth century, long before he justified their authority by deriving it from the that of the emperor. Neither he nor other Roman lawyers seem to have been concerned with compensation. In the north, on the other hand, Beaumanoir included the need for *soufisant eschange* when he allowed the count of Clermont to take property needed for

---

4. See, e.g., Accursius on Digest XL.11.5, quoted by Cortese, *La norma*, 1:128 (with a slightly anachronistic reference to *dominio eminente*), with other examples, ibid., 121, 137–38, 257–68; Guillaume de Plaisans, quoted by Dunbabin, "Government", 490 n.; Bartolus, *Opera*, 1:10 (Dig. Vet. Prima Const. Omnem).

5. Bartolus, *Opera*, 1.10, (Dig. Vet. Prima Const. Omnem); Woolf, *Bartolus*, 46, 118, 159.

6. Cortese, *La norma*, 1:268.

*le commun pourfit.*⁷ Perhaps the glossators and their successors, the postglossators, omitted it because it was not mentioned in the particular texts they were commenting on and, anyway, they took it for granted.

None of these comments or discussions went to the heart of the relation between property rights and collective rights: medieval lawyers seem to have followed their Roman and early medieval authorities in seeing property and government as originating together as a result of greed or more general sin. They do not seem to have been concerned about their relationship with each other or with the problems of expropriation. The common, unargued assumption about the priority of the common good suggests that the reason rulers had authority to expropriate was that a ruler was supposed to care for the community he ruled and to rule in the interests of the common good.⁸ In Kenneth Pennington's words, "Unarticulated norms permeate medieval juridical thought."⁹ Since discussions of the right to expropriate started from Roman texts about the emperor's rights, it is not surprising that they concentrated on expropriation by a prince or ruler rather than by a community. The way Bartolus stretched the idea of the prince to cover the community of an independent city may, however, support the possibility, suggested in earlier chapters, that lesser communities and lesser lords, in whom most jurists were not apparently interested, may have been making their own expropriations on their own authority. My impression, based on a limited survey of the sources and the commentaries of legal historians, is that most scholastics who discussed expropriation after Bartolus concentrated on the rights of the prince rather than that of cities or other lesser communities. One exception, writing in the early seventeenth century only just before Grotius, was the Spaniard Jerónimo de Cevallos, who considered whether both the prince

7. See chapter 3.3 and 3.4.
8. See chapter 5.2.1.
9. Pennington, *Prince and the Law*, 63.

and a free city could take the property of subjects by their public authority (*propter publicam auctoritatem*).[10] If it is right that this was rare, that leaves open the question whether the trend toward the reservation of expropriation to central governments was the result of the increasing influence of university-trained lawyers or whether academics were reacting to the increasing centralization of government.

If, as I argue, medieval expropriations were justified by appeals to the common good and by the assumption that rulers (at whatever level) were responsible for it, then there is no need to see the ruler's right to expropriate as deriving from a superior property right in the way implied by models of "feudal hierarchy." That need not mean that it was never envisaged in that way. Rulers, and most notably the kings of England, did indeed have other rights over some of the property of some of their subjects, according to their position in what was most clearly in England a hierarchy of property rights.[11] Medieval discussions of expropriation seem, however, to have paid as little attention to the status of different pieces of land as did expropriations in practice. Late in the twelfth century or early in the thirteenth, Azo decided that, according to an ordinance of Frederick I incorporated in the *Libri Feudorum*, the foundation text of the academic law of fiefs, Philip Augustus was wrong to seize Brittany from Arthur, who was Philip's vassal in the language of that law.[12] The arguments he cited on Philip's side before deciding against him included the public good, since taking Arthur's land enabled Philip to make peace with the king of England. This justification would have applied equally well outside the law of fiefs. As Azo remarked, the public good made many things lawful. In the fourteenth century, Bartolus's most

---

10. Pacheco Caballero, "La recepción hispánica," 182.
11. Reynolds, *Fiefs and Vassals*, 480.
12. Azo, *Die quaestiones*, 86–87; Lehmann, *Das Langobardische Lehnrecht*, 181 (II. 55); *Diplomata Regum et Imperatorum: Dip. Friderici I*, no. 242. On the *Libri*: Reynolds, *Fiefs and Vassals*, 215–30.

distinguished pupil, Baldus, maintained that fiefs could not be confiscated except for proved crimes, but that was the only cause for confiscation he mentioned, and he mentioned it because he was commenting on the law of fiefs:[13] other property was also forfeitable for crimes. The crime of treason (*infidelitas*) had incurred severe penalties, including confiscation, long before fidelity had the exclusively feudo-vassalic connotations that some modern historians have given it.[14]

The way that twelfth-century jurists began to divide *dominium* into *dominium directum* and *dominium utile* has been seen as a response to the need to adapt the supposedly absolute and undivided property of Roman law to the layers of property and jurisdiction that historians have seen as peculiar to the "feudal Middle Ages."[15] It is true that the first recorded reference to the difference between *dominium directum* and *dominium utile* is thought to have been made in comments on the twelfth-century *Libri Feudorum*. That, however, was itself an academic work, which soon became closely connected with Roman law, rather than a statement of the kind of feudal law that is traditionally supposed to have developed in the early Middle Ages out of Germanic law.[16] The use throughout the Middle Ages of the single word *dominium* for all kinds of authority and power, including both property rights and jurisdiction, does not mean that medieval people, whether academic lawyers or others, could not tell the difference between them. In the story about Martinus, Bulgarus, and the emperor's horse, Martinus apparently did not see the distinction, but most glossators and postglossators were against him. In restricting the ruler's

---

13. Baldus de Ubaldis, *In Usus Feudorum*, fol. 11, quoted by Canning, *Political Thought of Baldus*, 82.

14. Pollock and Maitland, *History of English Law*, 2:515 n.; Reynolds, *Fiefs and Vassals*, 422.

15. On property in classical Roman law: Schulz, *Classical Roman Law*, 338–42; Frier, *Landlord and Tenant*.

16. Feenstra, "Les origines du dominium utile," and "Dominium utile est chimaera."

power over his subjects' property, they took the distinction for granted. In thirteenth-century England, the Quo Warranto proceedings show that it was clear to non-Romanist lawyers and, presumably, to some laymen who had to defend their jurisdictions, even though the story of an earl coming into court with a rusty sword to vindicate his rights from the Conquest suggests that not everyone appreciated it.[17] In any case, jurisdiction was often in practice attached to landed property, and the boundary between them could be blurred.

The division of *dominium* in the sense of property rights was less a way of understanding the problems of property law in practice than a nice subject for academic argument. Bartolus made the original, twofold division into three by adding *quasi-dominium*, and others elaborated further, until Konrad Summenhart (1465–1511) produced twenty-three categories of *dominium*. At first most discussions of divided *dominium* seem to have concentrated on what might be called "property rights," with lesser jurisdictions attached, rather than on the *dominium* of kings or other supreme rulers. In the thirteenth century, however, Marino de Caramanico, defending the authority of the king of Sicily against the pope whose *feudatarius* the king was, maintained that within the kingdom the king was *dominus superior et supremus*.[18] Summenhart's twenty-third category of *dominium* was high or superior (*altum seu superius*), like that of a king. The Spaniard Francisco de Vitoria (1492–1546), citing Summenhart, used the expression *dominium eminens . . . et superioritas* for the power of princes or supreme rulers.[19] Grotius would later make the words *dominium eminens* famous, but Robert Feenstra, who remarked Vitoria's use of them and elucidated the origins of Grotius's ideas on property most thoroughly, thought that Grotius had probably not read Vitoria.[20]

---

17. Reynolds, *Fiefs and Vassals*, 361.
18. Quoted in Brett, *Liberty, Right and Nature*, 21 n.
19. Vitoria, *Comentarios*, 3:65.
20. Feenstra, "Der Eigentumsbegriff," 219, and "Expropriation," 144 n. 61.

Although drawing an extra distinction between a supreme ruler's authority and that of holders of subordinate kinds of *dominium* made the categories of *dominium* relate better to political realities, they do not seem in most discussions to relate very well to the varying rights and obligations attached to land in practice. They do not, in any case, seem to have affected ideas about expropriation.

The admittedly small selection of scholastic works, or modern works about them, that I have consulted concentrate on the right of rulers to take property rather than on the common good for which they were to take it. When the public or common good is mentioned, it is more often as *publica utilitas* or *communis utilitas* than *commune bonum*; but either way, as Pennington points out, the common or public good "was commonly used to justify actions that were not normally licit."[21] In itself, and in the context of expropriation, the common good seems to have needed no analysis or justification. Nor does the difference between *bonum commune* and *utilitas communis* seem to have been significant in this context. To theologians it could be important to distinguish what was morally good (*bonum*) from what was merely advantageous or useful (*utile*). At least one fifteenth-century canonist used the two phrases differently,[22] but for those who discussed expropriation the distinction seems to have been irrelevant. The crux for them was the right to take.

Though there may well have been discussions and justifications of expropriation (apart from confiscations for crime) that I have missed, my impression is that there was no significant development in ideas about it before Grotius.[23] In the fifteenth century, the problem of the rights to true *dominium* of heretics and infidels

---

21. Pennington, *Prince and the Law*, 23.

22. Kempshall, *Common Good*, 10–25, 54–64, 100, 115, 127, 202, 339–49; Pennington, *Prince and the Law*, 235–36; for other examples from treatises: Hibst, *Utilitas Publica*.

23. Examples of standard views: Pierre d'Ailly (d. 1420), quoted by Oakley, *Political Thought of Pierre d'Ailly*, 50–51 and n.; Paulus Castrensis (d.

that had exercised canonists since the thirteenth century became a matter for wider discussion, particularly in Spain and particularly in connection with conquests in America. Discussion seems to have focused more on the *dominium* of infidel rulers than on that of their subjects, so that it is relevant rather to the history of international law than to that of expropriation.[24] Francisco de Vitoria and Bartolomé de Las Casas both maintained, against much opposition, that infidel rulers could have true *dominium*. They both started, in an entirely conventional way, with natural law and the origin of property and maintained that rulers had only jurisdiction over their subjects. Las Casas added that their power and jurisdiction were justified only for the common good of their peoples (*ad procurandam utilitatem communem populorum*), and both made it clear that rulers could not take subjects' property at will. Neither seems to have felt the need to develop new arguments about expropriation in America, whether by native rulers or the Spanish.[25] They presumably thought that it would be subject to the same rules as expropriation in Christian societies.

As for any effects of the Reformation, though I have not found any elaborate justifications for taking church land, it could have been justified easily enough, as it had been in the Middle Ages, as done for the good of the kingdom concerned.[26] Philip Melanchthon allowed rulers to take subjects' property only for the common need (*gemeine not ... der Lande*).[27]

1447 or 1457), quoted by McGovern, "Private Property and the Jurists," 153; Vasquez de Menchaca, *Controversiarum*, fols. 25–25v (I.15.5), 164 (II.72.3); Suárez, *Selections*, 1:783 (VII.4.6).

24. Muldoon, *Popes, Lawyers*, esp. 133–58; Tierney, "Vitoria and Suarez."

25. Vitoria, *De Indis*, 232, 238, 254, 257, 265–66 (*Relectio* I.1.24, II.2, 16, III.1, 16); Las Casas, *De Regia Potestate*, 24–27, 33–37, 50, 56–58, 61, 91 (I.3–5, II.9.1, 11.3, 12, 23–24), and *Los tesoros*, 52–59, 322–26, 349–52; Tierney, *Idea of Natural Rights*, 257–65, 280; Fernández-Santamaria, *State, War and Peace*, 78.

26. See chapters 2.3 and 3.2, 3.4, and 3.6.

27. Melanchthon, *Opera*, 22:619.

94 ⁂ *Justifications and Discussions*

4.3 GROTIUS AND AFTER

The significance of Hugo Grotius (1583–1645) in the history of expropriation is not that he made any new rules about it: those he laid down reflected both tradition and the actual practice of his day. Nor was it that he introduced the expression *dominium eminens*, which would be adopted later in American law, though not apparently elsewhere, at least before this century, as a synonym for expropriation for the public good. What he said about expropriation was not merely a matter of words. Apart from the fact that he seems to have used the phrase rather differently from later American lawyers, the real importance of what he said about expropriation is that he constructed an argument that derived and justified the right of expropriation clearly from the origin and nature of all property rights.

In order to explain the nature and force of what would come to be called international law, which was the subject of his great work *De Iure Belli ac Pacis* (1625), Grotius started from the origin of civil society and government.[28] He envisaged individual people living simply under the law of nature in what his successors came to call the "state of nature." Everything was in common, and each could take what he needed, but this did not give security until people got together and agreed to form a civil society or community.[29] The law of nature said that one should not take from another what the other had taken for himself, but this did not provide adequate security of property (*proprietas*) until men formed a society in which they agreed, or could be assumed to have agreed, to submit

---

28. I cite the 1625 edition of *De Iure* by page number and, in parentheses, the book, chapter, and section. The unpaginated prolegomena is cited by a page number in square brackets.

29. Grotius, *De Iure*, [3–8], 6–7 (I.1.10), 138–41 (II.2.2). Grotius at different times uses the words *coetus, civilis societas, societas mutua, communitas, civitas, populus,* and *respublica* for the human communities or polities he discusses.

to civil laws, whether agreed by all of them, or the greater part of them, or those to whom they gave power.[30] As Grotius stated very clearly in his introduction to Dutch law, property (*eigendom*) was established by human communities (*menschlicke gemeenschaps*), so that each whole community had, and has, a higher right (*een hooger recht*) over the goods of its members.[31] There was nothing new in the idea of an original community of goods and the creation of property by convention and positive law: what, so far as I know, was new was the way that Grotius made it part of a chain of reasoning ending in the justification of expropriation for the common or public good.

Although for Grotius, in Knud Haakonssen's words, "Individuals with natural rights are the units of which all social organization is made,"[32] his reasoning nevertheless led to the effective subjection of individuals and their property to the communities to which they belong. The property of the members of any society can be taken by the ruler either by way of punishment or because of his *supereminens dominium*, exercised for the public good (*utilitas publica*).[33] As Robert Feenstra has pointed out, *eminens* or *supereminens dominium* was not for Grotius merely a right over the land of members of a community. It also covered the superior right that the community or its ruler had over the persons of its members, as well as over their property in general, including the right to tax it.[34] The right is to be used only for the public good (*ob publicam utilitatem*) for which people joined in civil society. The state (*civitas*) is bound to compensate those whose property is taken (*qui suum amittunt*). The way that Grotius wrote about

---

30. Ibid., 138–41 (II.2. 1–2, 4–5), 163 (II.3.19). Horne, *Property Rights*, 13–14, points to uncertainties about the priority of government or property.

31. Grotius, *Inleidinge*, 52; Feenstra, "Expropriation," 148.

32. Haakonssen, *Natural Law*, 28.

33. Grotius, *De Iure*, 4 (I.1.6), 163 (II.3.19), 308 (II.13.20.3), 316 (II.14.7).

34. Feenstra, "Expropriation," 137–43; Grotius, *De Iure*, 4 (I.1.6), 66 (I.3.6.), 723 (III.19.7), 734–35 (III.20.7.1).

eminens or *supereminens dominium* suggests that he reserved the right to expropriate to sovereign rulers, but this may not be what he intended any more than he probably would have intended, as a seventeenth-century Dutchman, to suggest that he thought of rulers as absolute monarchs. In his introduction to Dutch law he envisaged that local officials could take land when necessary, apparently on the initiative of their local communities.[35]

However much Grotius's ideas about natural law owed to previous writers, and however much his choice of the phrase *eminens dominium* owed to those who had written about the divisions of *dominium*, the way he combined them in an argument about the origin of society and property was new. All the ideas of the sequence of the state of nature, law of nature, and social contract that were developed in the seventeenth and eighteenth centuries seem to have originated with him. They are not as convincing now as they seemed then, but the way that Grotius fitted the traditional norms about expropriation into the sequence nevertheless made a more coherent argument about human beings, their polities, and their rights of property, than anyone had made before — or, so far as I can see, than anyone has since.

Some of the ways that Grotius's arguments about individuals and society were later used and adapted will be discussed in chapter 5. Here what is to be sketched briefly is the way that his contemporaries and successors regarded his justification of expropriation. *De Iure Belli ac Pacis* quickly aroused interest, partly, of course, for what it said about international law, partly for its whole argument about the formation of civil society, but also in some cases for the particular subject of expropriation. Scholars in the Netherlands and Germany soon began to argue about different parts of his thesis.[36] Wilhelm Leyser, for instance, maintained that individuals acquired property by their own will, not by contract, whether explicit or tacit. Some commentators thought that the words

35. See chapter 3.5, at n. 135.
36. Surveyed by Feenstra, "Expropriation," 148–52.

imperium eminens would be better than *dominium eminens*.³⁷ Samuel von Pufendorf (1632–94) pointed out that words mattered less than the powers they denoted. In his *De Iure Naturae* (1672) he seems to have used *dominium eminens* to cover the ruler's authority over property (including movables and money) rather than, like Grotius, over everything else. This was perhaps partly because he had started his first discussion of the subject, published in 1660, by distinguishing the types of *dominium* as *eminens, directum vulgare*, and *utile*. He followed Grotius's sequence of state of nature, law of nature, and the origin of property in compacts and consent, with modifications that left his justification of expropriation very like that of Grotius, though he seems to have been inclined to restrict it to cases of the urgent needs of the community (*res publica*).³⁸ In 1737 Cornelius van Bynkershoek, though he started by referring to *dominium eminems vel supereminens*, preferred to write of *imperium eminens*, as he thought that the word *imperium* distinguished the *potestas* of rulers from the *proprietas* belonging to individuals (*ad singulos*).³⁹ Whatever he called it, he, like Grotius, considered it to include power over the persons and goods of subjects, as well as over their land. He thought that distinguishing the degrees of necessity or utility could lead to mere quibbles over words, but he was slightly doubtful whether mere beautification of public areas ought to justify expropriation.

Dominium eminens seems to have been used increasingly to denote only the power to expropriate, rather than in Grotius's wider sense, though when writers were discussing expropriation it is not always easy to be sure that that was all it covered. Two Swiss writers of the midcentury, J.-J. Burlamaqui and Emerich de

---

37. Meyer, *Das Recht der Expropriation*, 125–27: I have not seen most of these works.

38. Pufendorf, *Elementorum Jurisprudentiae*, 1:24 (I.5.2–3); *De Iure Naturae*, 875–76 (VIII.5.7); Buckle, *Natural Law*, 53–124.

39. Bynkershoek, *Quaestionum Juris Publici Libri Duo*, 290 (II.15): this is obscured by the translation of 1934, which renders *imperium eminens* as "eminent domain."

Vattel, are particularly worth mentioning here because they seem to have been read a good deal in America. Both used *le domaine eminent* for the sovereign's right to take property, and not only landed property, from citizens, and derived the right, in what was by now the standard way, from natural law and the formation of civil society. For Burlamaqui property could be taken in urgent need (*dans un besoin pressant*), for the preservation and advantage of the state; for Vattel, in case of necessity and for the public welfare (*pour le salut publique*).[40] At much the same time the German J. H. G. von Justi considered that it was unnecessary to invent the concept of "*Obereigentum (dominium eminens)*" for the duty of subjects to sacrifice their property to the state.[41]

In France Grotius's argument seems to have caught on more slowly. In the sixteenth century, Du Moulin and Bodin had both used a version of the division of *dominium* in their discussions of royal authority. Du Moulin had maintained that, despite the existence of allods, the greater part of the lands of the kingdom was known to be under the king's *dominium directum* (*de dominio directo regis*, and held of him whether or not directly (*mediate vel immediate*). The king was nevertheless universal lord, not as *dominus seu proprietarius* of his kingdom, but as its administrator, in respect of jurisdiction and for the protection of property.[42] During the seventeenth century the idea of the king's *directe* was used to support higher claims, culminating in Louis XIV's statement that kings had the full and free disposition of their subjects' goods, both secular and ecclesiastical, for the needs of the state.[43] Some French lawyers derived the king's right to expropriate from his ultimate lordship of all land in the kingdom, but this was not

---

40. Burlamaqui, *Principes du droit naturel*, 1:61–62 (I.4.8); 2:274–75, 287–89 (III.5.26–28); Vattel, *Le droit des gens*, 2:218 (I.20.244).

41. Justi, *Staatswirthschaft*, 1:383–84.

42. Du Moulin, *Prima Pars Commentariorum*, 78, 133, 135, 657, 661 (1.5.49; 3.4.8, 17; 68.1.5; 68.2.13).

43. Louis XIV, *Mémoires*, 1:209.

Justifications and Discussions ※ 99

generally accepted: the public good remained the usual justification, sometimes explicitly, sometimes by implication, with the traditional requirement of compensation.[44]

The lawyers of Provence took up Grotius's *dominium eminens* in the eighteenth century, though apparently without developing it further.[45] It does not seem to have been noted or used by the legal writers Jean Domat, Nicolas de la Mare, or T. J. Pothier in their discussions of expropriation for the common good (*pour quelque usage public, le bien public, l'utilité publique*).[46] Montesquieu reckoned that when men surrendered their independence to live under political laws they acquired liberty and property that could only be taken from them by law. This could reflect Grotius's ideas, but Montesquieu's account of expropriation otherwise looks entirely traditional, citing Beaumanoir rather than Grotius.[47] The article on *Domaine* in Diderot's *Encyclopédie*, while quoting Montesquieu, also cites Grotius and Pufendorf and defines *le domaine eminent* as the sovereign's right to take property for the public good in case of pressing need. Rousseau, also writing in the *Encyclopédie*, called property the foundation of civil society and referred only in general terms to the obligation to contribute to public needs.[48] In *Du contrat social* he made property start with the social contract, civil liberties, and civil laws, but though he said that the state became master of all its members' goods and that individual rights were always subordinate to the community's rights, he does not seem to have grappled directly with the problem of expropriation.[49] Nor, so far as I have found, did the revo-

44. Sée, *Les idées politiques*, 70–72, 136–38.
45. Mestre, *Un droit administrative*, 297–332. See chapter 3.4, at n. 108.
46. Domat, *Les loix civiles*, 1:51–52; La Mare, *Traité de la police*, 4:10–12, 158–59; Pothier, *Traité du contrat de vente*, 2:31–33.
47. Montesquieu, *L'esprit des lois*, 1:5 (I.2), 2:222–24 (XXVI.15).
48. Diderot and Alembert, *Encyclopédie*, 5:19–20, 337–49; *propriété* (ibid., 13:491) is also noncommittal.
49. Rousseau, *Oeuvres*, 3:355–56, 364, 370 (I.4, 8–9; II.2); cf. ibid., 936 (*Projet pour . . . la Corse*).

lutionaries in and after 1789 find it necessary to rethink either the traditional justification of the common or public good or the traditional compensation. Once "feudal" and ecclesiastical property and rights had been got rid of, other property could be regarded much as it had been. The 1789 Declaration of Rights, while declaring property an inviolable and sacred right, allowed it to be taken when legally established public necessity (*la nécessité publique légalement constatée*) required it and for just and prior compensation. In 1793 the new clause defining the right of property (no. 16) was presumably the result of the revolutionaries' arguments about it and especially about the enclosure of common lands, but the separate clause about expropriation (no. 19) does not suggest that it needed any new justification. Nor does the absence of any reference to expropriation for the public good in the 1795 constitution, despite its new section on the duties of citizens, which included a clause (no. 8) reiterating the importance of landed property.[50]

Grotius was very soon read and admired in England, but only Hobbes and Locke among his early readers seem to have made use of his argument about the state of nature and the social contract, and neither of them followed him in connecting expropriation to the origin of property. For Hobbes the authority of the sovereign left no room for the protection of property against him.[51] Locke's argument about property is important because of his influence, not least in America. Yet it is much less cogent than that influence might suggest. For Locke, men enter civil society to protect their property — that is, their life, liberty, and estates — so that property seems to have started in the state of nature.[52] His argument that it is founded in labor is full of problems, not least because

---

50. Livesey, *Making Democracy*, 132–58; Roberts and Hardman, *French Revolution Documents*, 1:68, 173 (c. 17); 2:140–41 (cc. 16, 19), 340 (cc. 5, 8).

51. Hobbes, *Leviathan*, 101, 125, 172, 224–25 (cc. 15, 18, 24, 29); Tuck, *Hobbes*, 20–23.

52. Locke, *Two Treatises*, 301–20, 365–66, 368–70 (II, §§22–51, 119, 123–27).

it is difficult to see how "the turfs my servant has cut"[53] become mine, rather than the turf cutter's, in a state of nature, unless the property in another's labor is the kind of property that could exist in the state of nature.[54] Civil society having been formed by everyone's consent, laws should be made by all the members of the community or their representatives, or a majority of them.[55] This includes laws about property, but governments cannot take property from anyone without "his own consent — i.e. the consent of the majority." That individuals lose their property at the will of the majority does not fit very well with their entry into civil society so as to protect their own individual properties.[56] The requirement that individuals can take for themselves any land held in common only with the consent of all their fellow commoners, on the other hand, fits the actual practice of enclosures in Locke's day even worse.[57] That Locke, like many of his readers, was more concerned with taxation than with the taking of land may explain part of what seem to me weaknesses in his argument, but, though he cited both Grotius and Pufendorf, it is certainly weaker than either of theirs.

The *Oxford English Dictionary* has no example of the use of the term "eminent domain" in the eighteenth century, but one of "eminent dominion", which Sir Jeffrey Gilbert, a legal writer and baron of the exchequer, seems in his history of the exchequer to have seen in terms rather of the king's rights over his tenants under "the Feudal Law" than of expropriation in general.[58] The actual words "eminent domain" were, however, used in English in translations of works on natural and international law, though the translator of

---

53. Ibid., 307 (II, §28)
54. Ibid., 307–14, 317 (II, §§30–40, 45).
55. Ibid., 342–43 (II, §§87–89)
56. Ibid., 348, 378–80 (II, §§95, 138, 140).
57. Ibid., 310 (II, §35).
58. [Gilbert,] *Historical View*, 111–12; *Oxford Dictionary of National Biography*, 22:179–81.

Burlamaqui preferred "sovereign or transcendental propriety."[59] Blackstone did not use either phrase. His account of the subject is important for rather the same reasons as Locke's: his *Commentaries* were widely read. He says that private property was "probably founded in nature," though he is not very clear about how it came under positive law. He alluded to disagreements between Grotius and Pufendorf on one side and Locke and others on the other but sidestepped them as savoring "too much of nice and scholastic refinements!"[60] Natural law was a commonplace to be acknowledged, but English law was what mattered, even though Blackstone found it necessary to arrange the *Commentaries* in four books under the quasi-Roman headings of the rights of persons, the rights of things, private wrongs, and public wrongs.[61] Under "The Rights of Things" (book 2) he introduced a chapter on the "feudal system" in which he stated the "fundamental maxim and necessary principle (though in reality a mere fiction) of our English tenures, 'that the king is the universal lord and original proprietor of all the lands in his kingdom; and that no man doth or can possess any part of it, but what has mediately or immediately been derived as a gift from him, to be held upon feudal services,'" as "tenements" held by "tenants."[62] He said nothing in book 2 about expropriation, putting it instead in book 1 in connection with the right of property, which was one of the three absolute rights inherent in every Englishman. So great was the regard of the law for private property that it would "not authorize the least violation of it; no, not even for the general good of the whole community." A new road, he says, could not be made over someone's land without his consent, however, beneficial it might be to the

---

59. Burlamaqui, *Principles of Natural and Politic Law*, 2:211–12.
60. Blackstone, *Commentaries*, 1:138, 2:8 (I.1, II.1).
61. Lucas, "*Ex parte* Sir William Blackstone."
62. Blackstone, *Commentaries*, 2:51, 59 (II.4,5). For his views on the "feodal system" and English property law: Hargrave, *Collection of Tracts*, 498, cited by Lieberman, "Property, Commerce, and the Common Law."

public. "In vain may it be urged that the good of the individual ought to yield to that of the community." Yet he then goes straight on to say that "the legislature alone can, and indeed frequently does, interpose, and compel the individual to acquiesce," not "by absolutely stripping the subject of his property in an arbitrary manner; but by giving him a full indemnification and equivalent for the injury sustained."[63]

Blackstone's conclusion is thus entirely traditional and less determined by the peculiar liberties of the English than he may have intended to imply. The transition from absolute property, inviolate against the common good, to its frequent loss for the common good is perhaps to be explained by the lack of threat in his time or the recent past to the land of the kind of landowners Blackstone had in mind. The taking of land for the kind of public purposes that had long been accepted could be passed over fairly easily by an English lawyer who was not particularly interested in the work of continental writers on natural law and what they chose to call "eminent domain."[64] The kind of property right threatened by taxation was a different matter. When Blackstone turned from property in land to taxation, he was able to cite parliamentary victories and legislation. Given the different way that English common law treated landed and movable property, it might at first sight seem surprising that a writer as steeped in the common law as Blackstone should have included both land and movables — both the taking of land and the taking of taxes — under the single heading of "property." But here he was dealing with politics (in the form of the rights of persons) rather than with the complexities of English land law. That he was able to discuss expropriation so easily in what Maitland, in the context of Blackstone's feudalism, called "his easy attractive manner,"[65] is testimony to the lack of controversy about the principle of expropriation for the general good in

---

63. Blackstone, *Commentaries*, 1:138–40 (I.1).
64. Birks, "Roman Law Concept," 12; Mann, "Outlines," 204–5.
65. Maitland, *Constitutional History*, 142.

eighteenth-century England as well as to Blackstone's certainty about the blessings of the English constitution. The combination of absolute property in book 1 with everyone holding their property (even if by a mere fiction) as tenants of the king in book 2 is also a result of the recent past, in which the "feudal system" had become an essential part of political and legal history.[66]

One might expect that Scottish legal writers, with their training in Roman law and its medieval appendix on the law of fiefs, would have made more use of foreign works on law and politics. The few references to expropriation I have happened on have, however, produced rather minimal results. Stair's *Institutions of the Law of Scotland* (first published 1681) has only a brief allusion to the origin of property and its liability to expropriation. Bankton's *Institute* (1751) refers to the supereminent right of the sovereign power of each nation over the property and possessions of the subjects, which was to be exercised, with compensation, for the public good when necessity or expediency required. Erskine's *Institute* (1773) actually refers to Grotius and his use of the term *dominium eminens* for the right of the supreme power to take property, with compensation, when the "public police" required, as, for instance, when a highway was needed through private property.[67] Neither Adam Smith's *Lectures on Jurisprudence* nor *The Wealth of Nations* seems to deal with the subject.

As the eighteenth century wore on, the English colonists in America became much concerned about their property and threats to their rights from the British government. What they thought of as their property included much more than their lands and goods. It included all the rights that they thought belonged to them as Englishmen, and so far as their material property was

---

66. Reynolds, *Fiefs and Vassals*, 7–8, and *Kingdoms and Communities*, xvi–xviii.

67. Stair, *Institutions*, 93, 306, 309 (I.1.29, 31–32; II.1.34; Bankton, *Institute*, 1:10, 504, 529; 3:51–52 (I.1.32–33; II.1.4, 3.1; IV.45, R5, 24); Erskine, *Institute*, 195 (II.1.2).

threatened, it was by taxation rather than expropriation.⁶⁸ The distinction between land and movables probably mattered less in America than in England, as English property law was modified and simplified in the colonies. So far as property rights were concerned, opinions on their origin differed, but those who read Locke may have found that his labor theories made better sense in America than in England.⁶⁹ Those like John Adams and Thomas Jefferson who read about the feudal law and feudal government wanted American land to count as "allodial," so as to distinguish it from land in England, where, probably following Blackstone, they thought all titles to land derived ultimately from the king. There is a paradox here, since it was in America, both before and after independence, not in Europe, that land was initially granted by government: most land in Europe does not seem to have originated in royal grants, and the idea that it had been, even in England after the Norman Conquest, seems to have been derived from the postmedieval historians who originated the idea of feudal law and feudal society.⁷⁰ That, however, if true, is of merely historiographical interest. Apart from resentment of the quitrents owed in some colonies to the Crown or the proprietor of the colony, of the manorial rights reserved for a while in some areas, and of the restrictions imposed in 1763 on purchases of Indian land, there is not apparently much evidence of worry about rights in land.⁷¹ Nor, to judge from the actual cases of expropriation that I

---

68. Reid, *Constitutional History*, 27, 144–45; William Scott, *In Pursuit of Happiness*; William Nelson, *Americanization*, 51, 120–21; Hutson, "Bill of Rights."

69. Jefferson, quoted in Hutson, "Bill of Rights," 62–97; Mayer, *Constitutional Thought*, 77–80; Franklin, *Writings*, 10:59; Bailyn, *Ideological Origins*, 27–28.

70. Adams, *Papers*, 1:118; Jefferson, *Papers*, 1:132–33; Reynolds, "Did All the Land Belong to the King?"; Marshall Harris, *Origin of the Land Tenure System*, 62–79; Cunningham, Stoebuck, and Whitman, *Law of Property*, 14–22.

71. Goebel, "King's Law," and "Courts and the Law"; Friedman, *History of American Law*, 58–68; Banner, *How the Indians Lost Their Land*, 49–111.

have found, is there evidence of serious objection to the principle of the subjection of rights in land, whatever their origin, to the common good.[72]

How much eighteenth-century Americans were influenced by European works on natural law is, I gather, a matter of dispute among historians of the period. Americans, or at least some of them, read more foreign authors on law than the British English seem to have done, but they seem to have used the works of Grotius and his followers more as authorities on the international law that was, indeed, the principal subject of most of the treatises than as justification for taking the property of citizens. For Americans the law on the seizure of enemy property, and notably that of loyalists in the War of Independence, was particularly important. Most of all, however, the writers on natural law did not so much provide the basis of arguments against the British government as offer intellectual and political background and stimulus.[73] Lawyers in particular may have found more stimulating education in the natural law writers to supplement their necessary training in everyday practice and what Goebel called "the cloying text of Blackstone."[74] I have not, however, happened on evidence before the 1790s that they found or needed arguments about the principle of expropriation. Except for an allusion to impediments to "new Appropriations of Lands," the Declaration of Independence has nothing to say about property after the rhetorical flourish of its splendid opening. It mentions tax but not rights in land within the colonies, or even quitrents, presumably because by then no one was paying them any more.

Some state constitutions and declarations of rights from 1776 on mentioned the taking of property for public use or public uses, generally in fairly similar terms, all referring to the need for

---

72. William Scott, *In Pursuit of Happiness*, 10, 21–23.
73. See, e.g., Bailyn, *Ideological Origins*; Reid, *Constitutional History*.
74. Goebel, "Courts and the Law," 275.

compensation, and two also mentioning the need for consent to taxation.[75] The words "public use" or "public uses" may have been suggested by the fairly frequent taking of land for roads, which were obviously for public use as well as for a more general public good. But since land had also been taken for public buildings, some of which (like a governor's house, a powder magazine, or a prison)[76] would not actually be used by the general public, the words were probably not intended to be more restrictive than the "public good" or "common good."[77] Nothing that the state constitutions or declarations said on expropriation stated any new principle. What was new was the systematic making of constitutions and the systematic statements of individual rights, even when they said nothing that needed new arguments or justifications. Then, in 1791, the Fifth Amendment, though it oddly does not mention taxation, repeated the need for compensation for property taken for public use. Despite the preoccupation of the Founding Fathers with property rights in general, it does not actually say that private property may be taken for public use. That was evidently assumed, provided compensation was made, and there was apparently little or no argument in the Continental Congress about the clause. Until almost the end of the century, Americans, like eighteenth-century Englishmen, do not seem to have seen any need to justify or argue about either the taking or the compensation.[78]

In the 1790s there is evidence, perhaps merely because records were improving, though perhaps also in part because expropriations were multiplying and provoking more disputes, that lawyers were using and citing the writers on natural and international law on expropriation. Lawyers or judges in two cases of 1796, in Penn-

---

75. Cogan, *Complete Bill of Rights*, 361–74.
76. Ely, "'That Due Satisfaction Be Made,'" 4.
77. On later disputes: Stoebuck, "General Theory," 589–90; Epstein, *Takings*, 161–81; Nedelsky, *Private Property*, 232–36; Taggart, "Expropriation, Public Purpose and the Constitution," 99.
78. Stoebuck, "General Theory," 575–83.

sylvania and South Carolina, used the expression "eminent domain" and between them cited Grotius, Pufendorf, Bynkershoek, Burlamaqui, Vattel, and Rousseau, as well as Magna Carta, Blackstone, and some English cases.[79] The Pennsylvania suit was about the seizure of enemy property, though allusion was made to expropriation of the property of citizens for public use, with compensation.[80] The case in South Carolina was directly about the taking of freehold for public use. An application was made to the court against the taking of land under a state statute, which was alleged to be unconstitutional since it was done without a jury, as well as about the arrangements for compensation. Against the applicants, the city recorder of Charleston argued that taking land for public use conformed to "a law coeval with civil society and sprung out of the necessities of mankind, when they entered into a bond of union.... Hence all nations, at least all civilized nations, had concurred in the exercise of this right of opening roads and highways wherever it was most convenient and proper."[81] He also pointed out that compensation had been paid in South Carolina in the past even when land was taken "solely for the use of the state for military men." The judges were equally divided, so that the applicants got nothing, but it is clear that the Grotian justification of expropriation, with compensation, for the common good, combined with English precedents, was accepted.

4.4 CONCLUSION

As far as I am able to determine, the only serious attempt at working out a justification for expropriation for the common good before 1800 was made by Hugo Grotius, when he related it to the

---

79. Dallas, *Reports*, 3:199–285; Bay, *Reports*, 2:38–62. Dallas, *Reports*, 2:304–20 (1795) does not use the words and only cites English authorities.

80. Cf. arguments of 1782 in *Journal of House of Delegates of Virginia*, 1:68.

81. For South Carolina examples of payment of compensation, see Ely, "'That Due Satisfaction Be Made,'" 4–5.

formation of human communities that were able to establish and enforce laws. None of his followers seems to have added much of significance to his arguments and neither, apparently, has anyone else since. What seems clear from the arguments of Grotius and his followers is that they did not consider the rights of the community and its ruler or rulers over the property of their subjects to be superior property rights but to be *governmental* rights to adjudicate and legislate about property and, if necessary, take it for the common good. That is made particularly clear in the work of those who preferred the word *imperium* to *dominium* but, though *dominium* had been introduced into the discussions of Grotius and Pufendorf from earlier arguments about the division of property rights, it is also clear that neither of them considered eminent domain to be, or derive from, a superior property right. Grotius, in any case, took eminent domain to cover governmental rights in general, rather than merely expropriation of land.

This needs to be noted because of a tendency of some lawyers and historians since the eighteenth century to think of the rights of European governments over property as somehow derived from what has come to be called "feudalism."[82] Whatever the implications of property rights in the word *dominium*, the history of expropriation in Europe suggests that that is mistaken. As for America, property rights, especially after 1763, were indeed often founded on grants of land by colonial and independent governments,[83] and some writers have been inclined to see eminent domain as a relic of feudalism.[84] The third edition of Lewis's *Treatise on the Law of Eminent Domain* (1909) and the seventh edition of Nichols's *The Law of Eminent Domain* (1973) nevertheless both took the line that the power of eminent domain is not a property

---

82. See, e.g., Marshall Harris, *Origin of the Land Tenure System*, 21–61; Mann, "Outlines"; Hecht, "From Seisin to Sit-in"; Banner, *How the Indians Lost Their Land*, 13.
83. Banner, *How the Indians Lost Their Land*, 107.
84. Stoebuck, "General Theory," 557–58.

right, to be justified by the government's reservation, whether "feudal" or not, of some kind of superior layer of property.[85]

I have said comparatively little about discussions of expropriation that do not seem to amount to serious justifications. That is partly because they tend to follow fairly standard patterns, if with some elaboration of real or hypothetical examples, and partly because much more has been written on them by legal historians writing in the civil law tradition. There does not seem much point in my attempting to repeat or summarize what they have said.[86]

The limited nature of the justifications of expropriation before Grotius is more understandable than the lack of it since his day, during a period when ideas of universal human rights and capitalist ideas of property might both be expected to have made it harder to justify. That, however, I shall discuss in the next chapter, though even there I shall barely go beyond 1800.

---

85. Lewis, *Treatise on the Law*, 1:6–21; Sackman, *Nichols' The Law*, 7–22, 68–69.

86. See, e.g., Ugo Nicolini, *La proprietà*; and essays by Pacheco Caballero, Waelkens, and others in *L'expropriation*.

CHAPTER 5

Communities, Individuals, and Property

5.1 THE PROBLEM

In chapter 1 I remarked on an apparent lack of interest in expropriation for the common good on the part of historians of political thought, even those concerned with periods when the rights of property were much discussed.[1] Most historians of expropriation have correspondingly had little to say about the political ideas and assumptions that are likely to have underlain the subjection of individual property to collective needs.[2] The account I have given in chapters 2 and 3 of expropriation in practice, and in chapter 4 of the rather scanty and superficial justifications of it, suggest that its relation to ideas and assumptions about the nature of social and political structures, and their rights and wrongs, needs further investigation. This chapter is intended less to report the results of a full investigation, let alone draw conclusions from it, than to open the subject for further discussion. The later part of the story, after Grotius, is particularly puzzling. All I can do is suggest problems that those who know the period and the texts better than I do may be able to solve.

---

1. See chapter 1.2.
2. Ugo Nicolini, *La proprietà*, is a partial exception, but Feenstra's essays on Grotius that I have cited, important and authoritative as they are, focus closely on the use of words.

I am not concerned primarily with the great texts of political theory: their authors have always tended to focus on problems, disputed points, and their own particular insights. Meanwhile the historians of political thought have naturally been most interested in those same aspects of the works they study, and sometimes especially in what seems to show the origin of modern ideas about politics and government. For any attempt to explain the acceptance of the principle of expropriation, the chief value of texts of political theory and legal doctrine is that they may reveal assumptions about their own societies and politics which even the most original thinkers share. Other texts, such as documents of government or law, or the writings of nonacademics who take their society's norms more for granted, may be equally or more revealing about such assumptions.

5.2.1 BEFORE GROTIUS: COMMUNITIES

I should like to be able to argue that until the seventeenth century the ideas about society and government that were held and expressed in many societies, inside and outside Europe, were based on assumptions about the right structure of society that started from knowledge of the polities in which those who held the ideas lived. The chief subject of discussion would have been what was thought right and wrong within their own societies. I cannot do that: my knowledge, however far I stretch it, is totally inadequate. I can nevertheless suggest, however tentatively, that what I have read seems to suggest that people's ideas about politics did not generally arise from the perspective of separate and equal individuals in anything like what in the seventeenth and eighteenth centuries was called the state of nature or from the universal, individual human rights of the twentieth and twenty-first. Instead people seem to have started with the way that they found their own societies and polities to be structured. For many societies we do not have texts of what historians of political thought consider political thought or political theory. The traditional way of tracing the history of political theory used to be to start with the Greeks, pass to the Romans, and then jump to the Renaissance. Medieval political ideas now attract more attention, but it tends to be concentrated on academic treatises from the twelfth century on. Recent work by those who look outside the treatises has, however, shown how much about ideas and assumptions can be deduced from other texts, including chronicles and documents of government and law, from both before and after 1100.[3]

Whatever Greeks in general, including those living in less structured and less well-recorded polities than Athens, may have thought about the origin and nature of their communities, some of those whose works have been preserved certainly developed or alluded to ideas of natural equality and various kinds of golden age without government. Plato even envisaged something like a social contract when governments were first instituted.[4] Even so, the city-state seems to have been the main focus of attention. Some of the Greek ideas about human society without government were transmitted to the Middle Ages through Cicero and other Roman writers, with important additions. For my purpose the most significant of these were ideas about different kinds of law and the origin of property; the words and concept of *utilitas publica*;[5] and myths about the foundation of Rome. Medieval writers defined and classified the law of nature or natural law in various ways alongside divine law. However they did so, something of the sort was central to most writing about politics, although it did not imply anything like the kind of connection of politics in civil society with the state of nature that was postulated

---

3. Janet Nelson, "Kingship and Empire," and *Politics and Ritual*, 91–116, 133–72; Goetz, "Regnum," and "Perceptions of 'Power'"; King, "Barbarian Kingdoms"; Fouracre, "Carolingian Justice," and "Cultural Conformity"; Wickham, *Land and Power*, esp. 121–99; Davies and Fouracre, *Settlement of Disputes*; Reynolds, *Kingdoms and Communities*, xii, xxxviii–xxxix.

4. Lovejoy and Boas, *Primitivism*, 7–16, 27–102, 164.

5. Gaudemet, "*Utilitas Publica*."

in the seventeenth century. Society without government, whether before the Fall, before Cain built a city, or before Moses gave the Hebrews law and judges, seems to have been intended as a bit of early history rather than a hypothesis about the essential nature of human beings that would explain their rights and obligations in existing society.[6] In the here and now, human law and government were essential and were the starting point of discussion.

Samuel had warned the Hebrews against having a king, which may have suggested that polities did not have to be monarchies.[7] Nevertheless, until the recovery of Aristotle — and, in spite of Aristotle, even afterwards — monarchy seems to have been accepted as the natural form of government for fallen man. Kings were needed because there were kingdoms.[8] Kingdoms were formed out of peoples (*gentes, nationes, populi*), and peoples were assumed to form natural communities of custom and descent. This is made clear in the many mythical histories that were invented to explain the origins of the peoples inhabiting medieval kingdoms or cities. Whether they followed the Roman model in making a people come from Troy, or made it come from anywhere else, all these stories (with the significant exception of one about the Florentines, which explains their discords by their divided origins) imply that each medieval polity was envisaged as a permanent collective unit.[9] It is this assumption that political units were formed of collective and permanent "peoples" that, irrespective of the content of any story of a people's descent or its

---

6. Carlyle and Carlyle, *History of Mediaeval Political Theory*, 1:45–100, 132–46, 2:41–49, 5:14–20; Markus, "Latin Fathers"; King "Barbarian Kingdoms"; Tierney, *Idea of Natural Rights*, 145 n.; Friedberg, *Corpus Iuris Canonici*, 1:11 (Gratian, I D. VI, c. 3, D. VII, c. 1, D. VIII, c. 1); Boas, *Primitivism*, has examples chiefly from the early Middle Ages.

7. 1 Samuel (1 Kings in the Vulgate Bible) 8:6–18 (KJV); Buc, *L'ambiguité du livre*, 246–83.

8. For an opposing argument (about the ninth century): Fried, "*Gens* und *Regnum*"; cf. Goetz, "Regnum," and "Perceptions of 'Power.'"

9. Reynolds, "Medieval *Origines Gentium*," and "Idea of the Nation."

choice by God, gives these myths their fundamental significance for the understanding of medieval politics. However altered in reality by conquests or migrations, each kingdom at the time any story was being told or retold was assumed to be bound together, not just by its present political unity but by the common descent, customs, and law of its inhabitants. Some of the same assumptions of common descent and law applied to lesser units of government. This was not argued about: as the myths of origin show, it was just assumed. Even Dante, for instance, who argued for a universal empire, recognized that peoples, kingdoms, and cities (*nationes, regna,* and *civitates*) had their own characteristics and needed their own laws. Though most of the myths in the form we have them were written after 1100, that need not mean that they were the result of new ideas of collectivity. Evidence of collective government in the earlier Middle Ages, as well as the earliest of the myths, shows that they were not.

There is really no evidence to support the traditional belief that society at any stage of the Middle Ages lacked any collective loyalties so that, as Maitland put it in his evidently rather reluctant attempt to define feudalism, "the main social bond [was] the relation between lord and man."[10] What I deduce from such chronicles, charters, and other records of medieval secular politics as I have read, as well as from treatises, is that, from the early Middle Ages on, kingdoms were generally held together as much or more by collective political solidarities as by personal loyalties to their kings.[11] Rather the same, or perhaps more, applies to lesser lordships, villages, and other units of government. Of course interpersonal links and loyalties were there and mattered, as they must in any political system.[12] But I maintain that they functioned within

---

10. Maitland, *Constitutional History*, 143, cited by Reynolds, *Fiefs and Vassals*, 20; further discussion of ideas of collectivity in Reynolds, *Kingdoms and Communities*, xlv–lvi.
11. Reynolds, "Secular Power."
12. Innes, *State and Society*, 259–63.

polities that were assumed to form communities and were fortified, whether more or less, by the solidarities, whether stronger or weaker, of those communities. Medieval ideas about secular politics seem thus to have started from collective groups that were assumed to coincide with units of government. Some kingdoms consisted of more than one people or nation, in which case each one might form a unit of government within the kingdom. That seems to have been acceptable because government came in layers, and so the peoples under it could be assumed to do the same: even quite small units of government, like counties or lordships, insofar as they had their own laws and customs, seem often to have been assumed to constitute given, natural units.

Government was supposed to be conducted at each level, from kingdoms down to small lordships and villages, whatever their degree of autonomy, on the assumption that their subjects formed communities of custom and law, though not, of course, communities of equals. As in many human societies throughout history, hierarchy and inequality were not incompatible with solidarity: in some ways the acceptance of inequality, by inculcating submission, may make solidarity easier. Both the way that charters and laws refer to consultation and the way that aggrieved subjects complained about injustice and lack of consultation imply that rulers, from kings down, were meant to rule justly and according to custom, taking counsel with their greater subjects. Coronation oaths reinforced the implicit contract between ruler and subjects. In practice, rulers did not always take or follow what was thought to be good advice about custom and justice, but collective action in politics was more than an ideal. Government and law depended on it at every level, especially in the earlier Middle Ages, the age of what Timothy Reuter called "assembly politics."[13] Assemblies of the greater men of a kingdom, a province, or a village were sometimes referred to as if they were the whole people. Sometimes they were said to consist only of all the great men (*maiores*), but

---

13. Reuter, "Assembly Politics."

it came to the same thing, since the rich and powerful were supposed to represent the whole community.[14]

After Reuter's "assembly politics" gave way to more continuous and systematic government, systems of election to assemblies were devised, first in towns, with layers of councils, and then in kingdoms, with their parliaments or "estates." This widened the range of those consulted so that they look to us a bit more like modern democratic systems, but the impression may be rather misleading. Elections seem to have been designed less to give a voice to more individuals than to improve the representation of the community as a whole. Rather than promoting equality, moreover, they made the different rights of different classes more explicit. It remained the duty, as well as the right, of the richer and more established men, whether in a kingdom, a province, a town, or a village, to rule in the interests of the whole community. That did not mean treating everyone equally but it did mean treating them justly, according to contemporary ideas of justice. Throughout the Middle Ages conflict between classes seems to have generally been taken to be the result of injustice and sin, not of inherently conflicting interests. Protection and promotion of the common good, whether it was called *utilitas communis*, *utilitas publica*, or less often *bonum commune*, was therefore supposed to be a primary object of government — along, of course, with the welfare of the church and of the king and kingdom, with which it ought to coincide. Explicit references to the common good multiply, I suggest, with the multiplication of written sources, rather than with the invention of new ideas of collective solidarity or new duties of kings to protect their people and judge them justly.[15]

The development of government and estate management in

---

14. See, e.g., Wallace-Hadrill, *Fourth Book of Fredegar*, 102 (c. 33); Janet Nelson, "Kingship and Empire", 229; Widukind, *Rerum Gestarum Saxonicarum Libri Tres*, 39, 63, 73–74 (I.26, II.1, 10).

15. See chapter 2.3; Janet Nelson, "Kingship and Empire"; Barnwell and Mostert, *Political Assemblies*; Reynolds, "Secular Power."

the later Middle Ages in some ways undermined older solidarities and assumptions about peoples, as new myths of the separate origin of nobles and peasants were invented to supplement, though they never entirely supplanted, the old myths about the origin of whole peoples.[16] But in other ways it reinforced solidarities. More effective government and more regular taxes demanded more consultation, so that parliaments or estates became more organized and were more often summoned. More bureaucratic government, far from superseding collective activity by its subjects, needed more if its orders were to be carried out locally. Rulers who went to war not only sent round written orders to raise armies but sent propaganda letters to raise support for their wars by abusing their enemies and stressing the demands of patriotism and loyalty. This is traditionally seen as the beginning of national solidarities or "nationalism," but the old myths about the origins of peoples and the long traditions of consultative and collective government suggest that political solidarities at the level of what might now be called nation-states were not in themselves new. What was new, I suggest, was the use of the new technologies of bureaucracy to reinforce the solidarities that all units of government, but especially kingdoms, had long been supposed to have.[17] As governments made more regular demands on more of their subjects there was even more need for what A. B. White called "self government at the king's command."[18] He was talking about England and saw the local collective activity he described as fostering democracy, but he could have made much the same point about other polities, large and small, not all of which have traditionally been seen as nurseries of democracy. Protests always needed justification, and armed revolts needed it more, while justifications may have become more difficult to make convincing as

16. Freedman, *Images*, 107–30.
17. Reynolds, *Kingdoms and Communities*, 272, 274–75, and "Idea of the Nation."
18. White, *Self Government at the King's Command*.

government became more structured and more demanding. All the same, the obligations of rulers to rule justly, effectively, and according to custom continued to be stressed and, along with the claims of rebels to be resisting injustice or incompetence, continued to imply something like a contract between the ruler and the community of his subjects.

From the time that one can find evidence about local communities in the earlier medieval West, they seem to have been liable to be held collectively responsible and punished collectively.[19] Long before they were granted formal liberties, or even if they never got them, towns and rural communities of any size did justice among their members, which meant both judging and making law. The degree to which lords loomed over this activity varied but, even when they loomed heavily, judgments were supposed to be made collectively and law was supposed to embody the custom of the community. When groups wanted to make collective complaints against other groups or against outside individuals, they did so, suing and being sued and being represented by some or all of their members. Whether, how much, and why either more condensed settlement or more local autonomy meant more solidarity are matters deserving further thought. When local communities began to get privileges, one can see that in at least some cases they got them by bargaining with their rulers, which involved acting collectively before they received the privileges. Those who negotiated on behalf of any group would generally be its presiding officials, together with other leading members. There do not seem to have been any rules about this, though practical politics must have meant that any important or controversial decision or action was best done by as many and as impressive members as possible.[20]

Increasing regularity and system in government and law do not seem to have affected assumptions about the legality of group

---

19. Reynolds, "History of the Idea of Incorporation."
20. Reynolds, *Kingdoms and Communities*, 34–36.

activity. As late as the thirteenth century, Henry III of England accepted that villages could litigate either through their lords or through three or four of their members.[21] Frederick Barbarossa's statement in the previous century that all jurisdiction and governmental authority were exercised by delegation from the emperor had made no distinction between authority exercised by individuals and by groups. Nor did the English Quo Warranto proceedings in the thirteenth century.[22] It is true that in 1313–14 an English justice did make the distinction, apparently on the grounds that a commune was not capable of liberty (*comuna non est capax libertatis*) and that a city (*citee*) could not exist if it had not been made by grant of the king. If *comuna non est capax libertatis* was an accepted maxim, which seems improbable, it could only have been in England.[23] It certainly was not assumed in France when in 1273 two local communities were defeated in cases in the Parlement of Paris because they were not allowed to count as what the court called communes: in one case, the men of Lyon had their proxy rejected because the court held that they had *nec communia nec universitas nec aliquod collegium*. The real reason surely was that was they were locked in conflict with their archbishop.[24] If the king had wanted to tax them he would probably have imposed a tax on the whole city, taking for granted both its collective responsibility and the authority of the leading townsmen to coerce their neighbors. In 1295, after a violent revolt at Laon (Aisne), the city was deprived of its town bell, seal, and chest (*archa communis*) as well as the whole right of community and *collegium*. In Italy

---

21. Ibid., 140–41, works cited there at n. 103, and Timbal, "De la communauté médiévale," 338, suggest this was generally accepted.

22. *Diplomata Regum et Imperatorum*, 10: *Friderici I*, vol. 2, no. 238; Reynolds, *Kingdoms and Communities*, 63 n., and *Fiefs and Vassals*, index, under "delegation."

23. Maitland et al., *Eyre of Kent*, 1:xxv, lxiv, 130–31; *Oxford Dictionary of Medieval Latin*, 1:397–98.

24. Beugnot, *Les Olim*, 1:933.

the vocabulary was different again. Bartolus (unlike the English judge of 1313–14) held that the people of a city, *castrum*, or *villa* did not need permission to be a *collegium*, because they were one under the *ius gentium*, even though under *ius civile* other *collegia* needed authorization.[25] As his remark suggests, it was not just a matter of words but of politics and of the different legal traditions that developed within different jurisdictions. Canon law treated churches and their chapters differently again. Insofar as lawyers and governments began to consider the nature of groups at law, it may have been because secular governments wanted to control or license gifts of land to the church and needed to decide what kind of institution or group needed a license.

It does not make sense to try to judge these apparent inconsistencies or anomalies according to modern legal definitions (such as they are) or to argue that any group described as a *universitas* or commune had more unity or rights than other groups. The word *universitas* was often used without any implication of political capacity or legal power, as when letters were addressed to all the children of Holy Mother Church as *universitas vestra* — all of you.[26] About 1300 some Pisan prisoners of war in Genoa had a seal with an inscription that called them *universitas carceratorum Pisanorum Ianue detentorum*. Why not? They wanted to seal a plea for release, the seal was the seal of all of them, and nobody had told them that only some groups had the right to a seal. The modern concept of the "legal personality" or "incorporation" of a collective group, with which the word *universitas* has been associated, depends on having a difference between what a group that is defined as legally incorporated can do and what any group

---

25. Cited (with a similar statement by Baldus) by Ullmann, "Mediaeval Theory," 288. The other sources Ullmann cites there seem to me to bear out my suggestion that it was subversion, or fear of it, that determined the boundary between legality and illegality.

26. Reynolds, *Kingdoms and Communities*, 61–64; cf. Michaud-Quantin, *Universitas*.

not so defined can do. If any group can own property, go before the law to defend it, and so on, then there is no need or room for incorporation. The need for the distinction, as the expression "legal personality" implies, arises from a belief that rights in law normally belong not to groups but to "persons," in the sense of individual human beings, so that it is necessary to treat groups — or some groups — as "persons" or bodies having "personality."[27]

What I have argued elsewhere and still believe is that the definition of corporate groups in general, based on any principle that distinguished them from other groups, was not made in any European legal system until long after the Middle Ages.[28] Its absence was not the result of a failure to see something that was there to be found and, according to some modern interpretations, was found by Innocent IV or by later medieval jurists. Medieval people did not confuse the rights of groups and their members. For most purposes the two were the same. When they were not, so that people needed to distinguish between the interests or rights of, for example, a town and those of its individual burgesses, they seem to have done so to suit the particular case, just as we know that they sometimes distinguished between the interests or rights of a bishop and his church or those of a king and the people of his kingdom. Distinguishing between the rights of a group and the rights of its members is not primarily a matter of intellectual subtlety. It is easily done in some cases, harder in others, but begins to be done regularly only when there are political and economic conditions in which people with power want to outlaw certain sorts of group and have lawyers to help them argue the case. Late medieval lawyers used the metaphors of bodies or persons to describe the groups that they thought lawful, but the metaphors look like nothing more than that. The lawyers did not mean that groups had to be assimilated to individuals in order to have rights and duties. What they had to be was respectable. Collective action at

27. Canning, "Corporation in Political Thought," 15.
28. Reynolds, "History of the Idea of Incorporation."

law, as in ordinary life and politics, was fine and taken for granted so long as it was not subversive.[29]

I have stressed what I see as the collectivist assumptions behind medieval thought about society and politics because the evidence of them has been obscured by two ideas about medieval politics and society that seem to me misleading. First there is the miasma of modern ideas about the non-Marxist version of feudalism, with its exclusive stress on interpersonal bonds between lords and what are called their vassals. The second is the tendency to associate community, collective activity, and collective solidarities with ideas of democracy and equality, especially equal political rights. That association owes more, I suggest, to nineteenth-century views of the *Ancien Régime* colored by nineteenth- and twentieth-century politics than to medieval evidence about medieval politics and society. Aristotle's views on the politics of the city-state, as well as what anthropologists have written about many non-European societies, must also cast doubt on the inevitability of the connection between collective solidarities and the kinds of equality that have been central to political arguments in the last two hundred years.

5.2.2 BEFORE GROTIUS: INDIVIDUALS

All this emphasis on assumptions of collectivity, collective interests, and collective activities is not meant to suggest that medieval people submerged their individual interests in their communities. They looked after their own private interests, quarreled with their neighbors, and sometimes resorted to violence for selfish reasons. It is nevertheless testimony to the givenness — the supposed naturalness — of kingdoms that very few rebellious nobles demanded formal secession so that they could form separate kingdoms. The assumption that kingdoms belonged to peoples that constituted

---

29. Machen, "Corporate Personality," 258–60; Nékám, *Personality Conception of the Legal Entity*.

natural units of custom, law, and government may explain how the Kingdom of France survived the eleventh century and the Kingdom of Germany (by then conflated with the empire) survived the fourteenth, fifteenth, and beyond.[30] How far down the social scale regnal solidarity went is hard to know, but service in or to armies, attendance at local courts, and so on may have helped it percolate a fair way down. However much we may sympathize with those at the bottom of medieval society, and however much they must often have disguised their real views before their masters, it seems to me rash to assume that their discontents were based on the kind of claims to equality and democracy that have been widely publicized since the late eighteenth century.[31] Such a claim needs argument rather than assumption. My impression is that, despite the recorded radicalism of a few rebels, most of them demanded justice according to existing norms and greater participation within existing structures rather than anything entirely new. A good many, like people at the bottom of other societies through history, may, whether reluctantly or without thinking hard about it, have accepted their subordination — if only their rulers would rule justly and according to custom.[32]

The church cared about individuals, their sins, and their salvation. Lay society and law also cared about what we would call their rights. Laws and charters make that clear. Early medieval law codes that imposed penalties for injuring others imply, especially when a penalty was payable to the injured or their relatives, that people had something like what we would call a right to be compensated for what was evidently considered a wrong act, even

30. Scales, "Late Medieval Germany."

31. James Scott, *Domination and the Arts of Resistance* is largely concerned with modern societies and does not really consider beliefs. Moore, *Injustice*, 89, assumes wider social gulfs and more rigid divisions in "stratified, preindustrial societies" than seem to me to fit the medieval societies I know anything about.

32. Freedman, *Images of the Medieval Peasant*, 295–300; Reynolds, "Secular Power."

though the right and the compensation varied according to the status of the parties.[33] Rules about the procedures by which the accused could clear themselves similarly suggest something like rights at law. Janet Nelson has shown how ideas of rights, however unfamiliar their expression, pervaded ninth-century texts.[34] Charters of liberties to towns and rural communities included clauses for the protection of individuals that probably represented what the beneficiaries thought they should always have enjoyed according to custom. A very early one, the royal charter secured by the city of Genoa in 958, confirmed to all the faithful men of the city the quiet and peaceful enjoyment of their property and exemption from billeting or requisitions by royal officials. The charter to Pisa in 1081 included procedures to protect citizens charged with offences against the king. When in 1152 Frederick Barbarossa declared that any traveler could graze his horse on the roadside, he was perhaps confirming something like a tacitly accepted right that had recently been challenged.[35] Whether it was a new or old right, it was a very general one, restricted by status only so far as one would need to have a horse, or at least have charge of one.

Magna Carta is often considered more exceptional than it was. It is exceptional in its detail and elaboration because it was granted to the subjects of a kingdom with an exceptionally centralized and powerful government, but its most famous clause merely stated what was already considered right, at least by subjects, and not only those in England. The king's commitment, in clause 39 of the 1215 charter, not to capture, imprison, disseise (i.e., dispossess), outlaw, or exile any free man without due legal process had been foreshadowed in concessions made in 1058 by the abbot of Nonantola (Emilia, Italy) to the people of his town. It found par-

---

33. Though status mattered less than nonmedievalists sometimes assume: see, e.g., Dagger, "Rights," 299.
34. Janet Nelson, "England and the Continent."
35. *Diplomata Regum et Imperatorum*, 10: *Friderici I*, vol. 1, no. 25, c. 20.

allels in promises made by kings of Castile and León in the twelfth and thirteenth centuries as well as in many later local charters, *Weistümer*, or statutes.[36] A ruler's promise not to do something implies that he has been doing it and that he now admits — however reluctantly and insincerely — that it was wrong. That a ruler's actions could be wrong and that wrongs should be put right implies that his subjects had something that we would call individual rights, even if not everyone had the same rights. That, indeed, would still be the case in practice even after the Rights of Man were proclaimed in the eighteenth century.

Despite this evidence that medieval societies recognized something like what we would call individual rights and thought about them enough to demand and bargain about them, historians of medieval political thought have sometimes suggested that the idea of natural or human rights is postmedieval.[37] That, I suggest, is because the treatises they study do not discuss the rights of individuals in the way that they have been discussed since the seventeenth century. They start from different premises, concentrate on different issues, and use different concepts and language to discuss them. John Finnis has argued that Thomas Aquinas sometimes used the words *ius* or *iura* to mean a right or rights, rather than a law, and at least some of his examples seem convincing — which is unsurprising to anyone accustomed to the use of *ius* for property rights in charters.[38] Irrespective of the words Aquinas used, moreover, all he says about the duty of a ruler to do justice, and of individuals not to harm each other, suggests that he envisaged individuals as having interests which amounted to some kind of rights that might be, but should not be, infringed.

What was more important to Aquinas when he wrote about

---

36. Reynolds, *Kingdoms and Communities*, 130–32; *Cortes de León*, 1:31–32 (VII, cc. 1,2,4), 140 (XXV, c. 1).

37. Views surveyed by Tierney, *Idea of Natural Rights*, 2–5; Dagger, "Rights."

38. Finnis, *Aquinas*, 132–38, 170–274.

politics, as distinct from theology, was nevertheless the given existence of political communities and of the duties of rulers and subjects within them. For Aquinas, despite his use of Aristotle, and although he must have been aware of nonmonarchical governments in Italy, monarchy was still the best form of constitution.[39] The need to follow the Latin translation of Aristotle made him describe the perfect or complete community as a *civitas*, but he qualified it by referring sometimes to a *civitas vel regnum*, a *civitas vel gens*, or a *civitas vel provincia*. Even Marsilius of Padua, however different his state may look from more conventional discussions of kingdoms and kings, could still not avoid mentioning kingdoms. They were there. They were the default form of government and the highest form of secular community. Discussion was bound to focus on the way they should and should not be governed and their laws should be made.[40] Academics articulated and analyzed the problems, but they seem to have started from much the same assumptions about justice, consultation, and judgment as did lay people, so far as I can deduce them from the records of government and law.

5.2.3 BEFORE GROTIUS: PROPERTY

The aspects of government, law, and rights that most concern the rights and wrongs of expropriation are the regulation, law, and rights of property. The general view of those who thought about such things in the Middle Ages seems to have been that property, like government and human laws, was the result of sin.[41] Government, law, and property (*dominium*) went together but apparently without the kind of discussion of their origins that could form the

39. Aquinas, "De Regno ad Regem Cypri," 451, 456 (I.2, 6).
40. References in Reynolds, *Kingdoms and Communities*, 322–23.
41. Carlyle and Carlyle, *History of Mediaeval Political Theory*, 1:45–100, 132–46, 2:41–49, 5:14–20; Friedberg, *Corpus Iuris Canonici*, 1:11 (Gratian, I D. VI, c. 3: D. VII, c. 1: D. VIII, c. 1)

basis of judgments about rights and obligations in the here and now. One thing seems clear: most free property does not seem to have been thought of as originally granted by a king. Early medieval nobles and free men did not generally hold their lands and owe services to their kings or lords because of a real or supposed grant of land to them or their ancestors. That does not mean their property in their lands was absolute, any more than any property can ever be.[42] But the services they owed seem to have been owed rather as subjects of their rulers and members of their communities than as what historians have called feudal vassals.[43]

Disputes about land, though sometimes settled by force and bullying, were supposed to be settled by collective judgments of those who seemed to represent the relevant community and know its customs. Although rights in land were matters of custom, they could on occasion be adjusted or changed by legislation, which was supposed to be done after consultation with suitable representatives of the community.[44] Property in land was thus subject to regulation and control by the community. This is most obvious at the local level, when local communities regulated the use of both common and arable land, and (in the case of some early medieval Spanish communities) even made collective gifts of land to churches.[45] Given the general lack or vagueness of categories and definitions in customary law, it is possible to envisage that all these subjections of landed property to communal control and regulation, including obligations to provide goods and services, such as entertaining the ruler or billeting his men in one's house (*mansionaticum, albergum, gistum, hospitium*)[46] may perhaps have shaded into obligations to give up one's land when the community needed it. Since the needs of defense of the kingdom or local

42. See chapter 1.1.
43. Reynolds, *Fiefs and Vassals*, 57–64.
44. Reynolds, *Kingdoms and Communities*, 18.
45. See chapter 2.5.
46. Not considered here; see chapter 1.1.

community explain the obligation to build, repair, and man fortifications, they could perhaps by extension also cover an obligation to give up land for them.

As government and estate management became more systematic and professional, kings and lesser lords used literate servants to keep records and employed lawyers of a new professional kind to support their increasingly regular demands for taxes, dues, and services. Jurisdictions began to be organized into more or less clear hierarchies of appeal and the boundaries between them were argued about and defined. Obligations on landowners became heavier and had to be more frequently fulfilled, while a new vocabulary of fiefs was introduced to denote their lands. It is not clear, however, that either the new obligations or the dominance of the new professional law with its new vocabulary significantly diminished the security of rights over their property enjoyed by landowners, or at least those of landowners with the political clout to argue with their rulers or the resources to pay lawyers to argue for them.[47] Academic and professional lawyers produced more arguments that in turn produced new distinctions, but, so far as I can see, no very revolutionary ideas about property rights in general. Whether or not the story about a twelfth-century discussion of the emperor's rights over his subjects' property is true, the glossators and postglossators of Roman law obviously found a problem in Justinian's texts that stimulated discussion. The consensus they reached seems to have left him merely with jurisdiction and what looks like only the traditional right to take property. In practice that probably meant taking it for something that could be presented as the common good.[48] The texts of Roman jurists that seemed to put the prince above the law were nearly always interpreted so as to deny that any ruler ought to have really absolute or arbitrary power. When they came to be interpreted differ-

---

47. Reynolds, *Fiefs and Vassals*, 64–73, and later chapters on particular countries; Reynolds, "Emergence of Professional Law."

48. See chapter 4.2

ently, it was because governments were becoming more powerful and ambitious rulers wanted suitable opinions from their lawyers. But it may have been changing practice that stimulated changing ideas, rather than vice versa. References to claims by kings to be above the law tended to be disapproving.[49] When absolute power began to be more openly discussed, most lawyers continued to hedge their statements about it. Ideas about expropriation meanwhile seem not to have changed significantly, any more than did its practice.

I cannot claim that the strongly collectivist character that I have attributed to medieval political ideas and activities entirely explains why expropriation for what was seen as the public good was as widely accepted as it seems to have been. If we did not have evidence of the practice it would be impossible to deduce it from the general ideas about politics that I have described. But I do claim that the practice is at least more explicable and understandable against the background of ideas about the collective character of society and politics, not least because so much of it seems to have been so uncontroversial.

5.3 GROTIUS AND AFTER

Since much has been written about the spread of new ideas in the seventeenth and eighteenth centuries by those who work on the period, I shall be more brief about them, concentrating only on the way that they seem to have affected rights of property and therefore expropriation for the common good. That is easy enough so far as Grotius and some of his followers are concerned but becomes harder as the eighteenth century wears on. It seems to me much more difficult to understand how expropriation for the common good fits into the ideas that have developed since

---

49. Pennington, *Prince and the Law*, 76–118, 202–37; Reynolds, *Kingdoms and Communities*, 46–51; Berend, *At the Gate of Christendom*, 176; Carlyle, "Some Aspects."

then than it is to suggest why earlier societies had taken it for granted.

Chapter 4.3 sets out the main outline of Grotius's argument, so I shall not repeat it here. As I said there, few of its component parts were new: what Grotius did was join them into a sequence that led from separate individuals in a state of nature through a contract that they made to form a society that would make property secure. Only in such a civil society would secure property and agreed law be possible. Because property thus came from society, society could take it away again, but only if it was needed for the common good that was the purpose of the contract and the formation of society. The political implications of starting from individuals were enormous. In the long run they changed the assumptions from which much political thinking started, but this did not happen at once. Traditional notions about the law of nature and the basis of government in a more or less contractual consent continued to be used in the traditional way by those who had either not read Grotius or took on only part of his ideas without following his full sequence.[50] Talk of contracts had already been becoming more frequent and explicit, but the broken contract on which some of the English Civil War pamphlets focus, for instance, looks like that between king and subjects, rather than the social contract by which individuals entered civil society.[51] Arguments about property in the Putney debates among the soldiers of the New Model Army, even when it was said to be "of human constitution" rather than given by the law of God or of nature, were about the political privileges attached to property, rather than any question of its subjection to community need.[52] Algernon Sidney read and admired Grotius but shaped the argu-

---

50. Christianson, "Political Thought in Early Stuart England"; Sommerville, *Royalists and Patriots*, 15–16, 62–65, 102.

51. See, e.g., Hooker, *Ecclesiastical Polity*, 1:187, 190–91 (I.10.4, 8); Thomason Tracts, no. 370 (12), 9, 26, 32; 378 (13), 17.

52. Philip Baker, *Putney Debates*, 73–80, 84.

ment of his *Discourses* in the traditional way around the liberties of the English.[53] While both Hobbes and Locke may have taken from Grotius the idea of starting with individuals in the state of nature, they both used it quite differently.[54]

By the eighteenth century the state of nature, social contract, natural law, and natural rights were commonplaces of political writing, although some adapted or rejected bits of them with varying degrees of cogency.[55] Increasingly, perhaps as a result of attacks on the idea of the social contract, attention came, so far as I can see, to focus more on individual rights than on their basis in the foundation of the community. Without the contract the difference between natural and civil rights may have seemed less significant. Some writers considered the more important individual rights to be natural rights that men brought with them into society and that ought to be preserved in society. For those who followed Locke, such rights included property, though Jefferson still thought it a "moot point whether the origin of any kind of property is derived from nature at all."[56] For some time and in some of these discussions, individual rights, even inalienable natural rights, were not apparently seen as dangerously revolutionary, even when expressed, as they were by Jean-Jacques Burlamaqui, in what would later become the revolutionary phrase *"les droits de l'homme."*[57]

It was, I suggest, the American Revolution that made individual rights both revolutionary and influential outside intellectual

---

53. Sidney, *Discourses*, 1:317, 382, 428, 2:82, 280, 317; Jonathan Scott, *England's Troubles*, 149.

54. Haakonssen, *Natural Law*, 31–35; Malcolm, *Aspects of Hobbes*, 458, 525–28; Bobbio, *Thomas Hobbes*, 149–54; Locke, *Two Treatises*, 22, 74, 86, 138, 143, 248 n., 306 n.

55. Riley, "Social Contract Theory."

56. Quoted by Griswold, "Rights and Wrongs," 174–75; Epstein, *Takings*, 5. For Locke on property, see chapter 4.3.

57. Burlamaqui, *Principes du droit naturel*, xiv, 123 (pt. 1.7, §4); Haakonssen, *Natural Law*, 311–21.

circles. By the 1760s the colonists' ideas about the blessings of the English constitution, law, and liberties had been supplemented by the newer and more abstract concepts developed by writers since Grotius. Fewer Americans probably read the continental followers of Grotius, let alone Grotius himself, than read Locke, but enough of them read enough to be able to use the ideas to construct arguments for their needs.[58] The way that they discussed natural law and natural rights, along with the way that they understood equality, probably explains how Jefferson could claim in 1776 as a self-evident truth that "all men are created equal, that they are endowed by their Creator with certain unalienable rights, that among these are Life, Liberty and the pursuit of Happiness."[59]

The bills of rights that the American states began to draw up seem to have derived the title from the English bill (or rather statute) of 1689, though that had dealt mainly with traditionally collective liberties, including relatively little on individual rights. It also said nothing, despite a clause on taxation and another against "excessive fines," on property in general, let alone the taking of land.[60] Opinions differ on the extent to which either these state bills, or the federal bill, which was being debated in 1789, influenced the Declaration of the Rights of Man which the French National Assembly was debating and passing at just that time. It is, however, hard not to infer from Jefferson's correspondence with Lafayette and Madison that the American documents formed at least one significant source of inspiration among others.[61] All

---

58. Bailyn, *Ideological Origins*, 26–29, 34–45, 58–59, passim; Hutson, "Bill of Rights"; Haakonssen, *Natural Law*, 310, 322–41.

59. Greene, *All Men Are Created Equal*.

60. 1 William and Mary, sess. 2, c. 2, in *Statutes at Large*, 3:440–43; Hutson, "Bill of Rights"; Levy, *Origins of the Bill of Rights*, 5. The list of charges against George III in the Declaration of Independence evokes those against James II.

61. Fauré, *Déclarations de droits de l'homme de 1789*, 312–15; *Archives parlementaires*, ser. 1, 8:221–22, 256–61, 427–32; Jefferson, *Papers*, 14:436–38, 15:165–68, 230–33, 268, 358, 364, 367–68, 385–87, 390.

these bills and declarations spread the idea of individual and equal natural rights, but its widest diffusion came from Thomas Paine's *Rights of Man*. Published in 1791–92, it sold perhaps a hundred thousand copies in America, two hundred thousand in England by 1793, and was rapidly translated into French and German.[62] Mary Wollstonecraft followed with *A Vindication of the Rights of Woman* in 1792. The *Oxford English Dictionary* oddly cites no examples of the phrase "the rights of man" and gives its first example of "the rights of woman" from the hostile Hannah More in 1799, thus omitting any reference to Paine or Wollstonecraft. By 1816 the concepts and the phrase were, however, commonplace enough for Jane Austen to refer ironically to the rights of men and women to have supper at a private dance.[63]

All this discussion of the rights of individuals, especially when they were taken to include rights of property, makes it harder to see how the collective rights of a polity over its members' property continued to be taken for granted, as they seem to have been, in law codes and constitutions as well as in practice.[64] Although some eighteenth-century writers went on using Grotius's sequence of state of nature, social contract, and civil society, the increasing emphasis, both in America and France, on individuals tended, quite apart from problems about the contract, to break or ignore the chain of his reasoning that ended in collective controls over property. It was not merely, or not so much, that Grotius's argument was found unsatisfactory as that, once his chain of reasoning was broken or forgotten, its relevance to expropriation was ignored. If the wider theories about politics, society, and individual rights had governed the practice of expropriation, it

---

62. Thompson, *Making of the English Working Class*, 117; Keane, *Tom Paine*, 307–8, 331; Quérard, *La France littéraire*, 6:646; Kayser, *Vollständiges Bücher-Lexicon*, 4:292; Craig Nelson, *Thomas Paine*, 220, 227–28.

63. *Oxford English Dictionary*, 13:924 ("rights," I.10a); Austen, *Emma*, chapter 29.

64. See chapters 3 and 4.

might have been questioned. Yet it seems not to have been even discussed.

Part of the explanation may depend on the survival, alongside the new theories, of the old ideas of natural, given political communities, whether they were called nations, peoples, or kingdoms.[65] Histories of nationalism often see such ideas as new, but they generally discuss them with little consideration of earlier assumptions about kingdoms and peoples and, moreover, do not always connect them with the newer and more intellectual ideas of the state of nature and individual rights. The old ideas of nations or peoples seem, nevertheless, to have coexisted with the new political ideas even in the minds of those who worked out the new ones. Grotius himself wrote about the freedom of the ancient Batavians as ancestors of the free people of Holland. He may well not have seen any incompatibility between the assumption of a continuous political community and his later arguments about the origin and authority of governments.[66] Perhaps there is none: it is simply a parallel story of a kind which, it is clear, many people, both learned and unlearned, continued to cherish.

New and old ideas could be combined in various ways. Edmund Burke dismissed the new, with scornful passing references to the rights of men and social contracts, while admitting the old kind of contract between king and people and referring to the English and French nations in an entirely traditional way. His occasional use of "us" for the past English underlines his assumptions about the long and continuous identity of the English nation.[67] Three notable exponents of the new ideas, on the other hand, Rousseau, Jefferson, and Emmanuel-Joseph Sieyès, all seem to have assumed the old idea of natural, given political communities alongside the new idea of communities formed by individuals with their indi-

---

65. See chapter 5.2.1.
66. Schöffer, "Batavian Myth."
67. Burke, *Reflections*, 104, 113, 150, 153, 194–95, 197.

vidual rights. Rousseau's ideas about the state of nature and the social contract, however idiosyncratic, clearly derive from the new paradigm. His ideas about nations clearly do not. He thought that peoples or nations had originated as communities of custom and way of life, although they were now under governments that he thought illegitimate. The actual nations or peoples he mentioned by name or seems to have had in mind were all long-established units of government. That includes Poland, even if it was now in trouble, and Corsica, even if it had been passed around between different states like a parcel: it remained a single parcel and one whose inhabitants, or some of them, had ideas about their own collective rights.[68] Rousseau's nations, in other words, were what would have been taken for granted within an older set of political assumptions as political communities. Jefferson started the Declaration of Independence with two paragraphs that offer a concise combination of the old and new sets of ideas. Before proclaiming the equality and rights of all men as self-evident, Jefferson referred to "one people" with political rights in a way that seems to reflect the old assumptions and needed no justification or explanation, even though his "people" had hitherto been connected by "political bands" with another. Sieyès's *Qu'est-ce que le Tiers-Etat?*, which has been called the most celebrated pamphlet of the revolutionary period, suggests a more elaborate and perhaps more conscious combination of new and old. It declared that the nation was prior to everything but was formed by individuals joining together so as to have a common or national will and so form a government.[69] The nation on which he focused without hesitation was geographically coextensive with the Kingdom of France, though he counted only the Third Estate as its citizens. In

---

68. *Oeuvres complètes*, 3:169 (*Discours sur l'origine de l'inegalité*, pt. 2), 381–83, 386, 391 (*Contrat social*, 2.7, 8, 10); Barnard, "National Culture and Political Legitimacy."

69. Sieyès, *Qu'est-ce que le Tiers-Etat?*, chapter 5; K. M. Baker, "Political Languages," 629–30.

seeing the nation as "a primordial reality," Sieyès was redefining the nation and prefiguring a reshaping of its political structure, rather than inventing it as a political community. That was already a given.

From now on the old idea of nations or peoples as natural, given communities was combined with the new ideas about individualism and political equality to become modern nationalism.[70] What is — or may be — relevant about it here is that the old ideas about the solidarity of peoples or nations, just because they were so unexamined and taken for granted, provided the cohesion that polities composed of supposedly equal individuals needed to hold them together. It may be that this helped to maintain the old acquiescence to the principle of the surrender of individual property when it was needed by the community, however contested it might be in individual cases. That is only a very tentative hypothesis: there seems to have been so little discussion, even in the course of composing declarations, codifications, and constitutions, about the principle of expropriation for the common good, that it is very difficult even to guess how it was considered to fit into wider principles. The idea of the state or nation as composed simply of individuals meanwhile made the anomalies and contradictions about group action at law that had accumulated since the later Middle Ages even more glaring. Long and tortuous arguments about the legal nature and capacity of groups took place, resulting in the invention of various — not very satisfactory — concepts of legal personality or incorporation.[71] Yet no one seems to have thought that the clash between individual property rights and expropriation needed similar discussion and resolution. Even Madison, who drafted the Fifth Amendment, did not apparently find problems in its last sentence that needed much argument.

70. Reynolds, "Idea of the Nation."
71. Reynolds, "History of the Idea of Incorporation."

If it is right — and it may not be — that no one either in France or the United States on the one hand, or in the less revolutionary states of Europe on the other, felt any need to fit expropriation for the public good into their wider ideas about politics, the chief reason may have been simply that the practice was both well-established and essential to their functioning. No polity with individual rights of property in land could dispense with it entirely. The polities of 1800 were about to need it even more than they already did.

5.4 CONCLUSION

I have argued that it is relatively easy to understand how expropriation for the public good was taken for granted in Europe (and, I tentatively suggest, elsewhere) before the seventeenth century. The problem of integrating it into wider political theories in the seventeenth and eighteenth centuries remains puzzling. Others may explore it further and take the subject into the nineteenth and twentieth centuries. While property itself came under much more serious and radical attack after 1800 and was defended with increasing vehemence, expropriation for the public good became the subject of much legal argument. Individual cases were contested and some general rules and procedures were worked out in different jurisdictions. In the United States — though apparently nowhere else — the subject was dignified by the name of "eminent domain." Yet, despite all the legal arguments, the political implications and justifications of the principle seem to have been relatively little discussed, at least in the works that I have happened to find. The subject seems to have generally been left to the lawyers.

This may seem an unsatisfactory conclusion on which to end. Others may be able to resolve the problem of modern ideas that puzzles me. In a way, however, the very irresoluteness of my conclusion illustrates the wide acceptance of expropriation for the public good: the question of its political implications and justification may remain open, at least in part, because expropriation has been so much taken for granted that it seems not to have needed discussion. During the centuries when polities were assumed to form natural, given communities into which individuals were born, the problem of reconciling rights of property with the needs of communities hardly arose. It should have become more noticeable when ideas of politics and society started from separate individuals with universal human rights. The sanctity of property rights then began to be more stressed; and then, by an irony of history, canals, railways, roads, and airfields began to need more and more land to be taken. Yet no writers seem to have tackled the contradictions head on.

Whether or not political thinkers in the past worried about the way that their societies reconciled individual property rights with collective needs, it remains a subject in which historians might care to take more interest than they have done so far. It poses a problem that this book has started to tackle, in the hope of stimulating others to go further. They may well find mistakes in it to correct and will surely be able to fill in some of the gaps in the stories of expropriation in the areas I have surveyed. It would be even better if those who work on the history of other parts of Europe and of other continents would look for evidence there. In some areas there may be little or none to find. Even where individuals have had rights in land, what they held may not have ever been taken from them for the common good. Even if it was, there may not be any records to show that it was. I nevertheless suggest that expropriation for the common good remains a question of comparative history that is worth examining.

Works Cited

ABBREVIATIONS

AHR	*American Historical Review*
AJLH	*American Journal of Legal History*
EHR	*English Historical Review*
FSI	Fonti per la storia d'Italia
HMSO	His Majesty's Stationery Office
MGH	Monumenta Germaniae Historica
RSJB	Recueils de la Société Jean Bodin

MANUSCRIPTS

East Kent Archive Centre

sa/ac 1	Black Book of Sandwich, 1431–87 (microfilm)

London, House of Lords Record Office

Microfilm of Public Acts: 9 Geo. I

London, National Archives

C 145	Chancery Inquisitions Miscellaneous
E 351	Pipe Office, Declared Accounts
SC 8	Ancient Petitions
SP 1	State Papers of Henry VIII

PRINTED WORKS

Acts and Resolves, Public and Private, of the Province of Massachusetts Bay. 21 vols. Boston: Wright & Potter, 1869–1922.

Adam of Eynsham, *Life of St. Hugh of Lincoln.* Edited by D. L. Douie and H. Farmer. Edinburgh: Nelson, 1961.

Adams, John. *Papers.* Edited by R. J. Taylor et al. 8 vols. Cambridge, Mass.: Harvard University Press, 1977–89.

Albert, William. *The Turnpike Road System in England, 1663–1840.* Cambridge: Cambridge University Press, 1972.

Allan, Colin H. *Customary Land Tenure in the British Solomon Islands Protectorate.* Honiara: Western Pacific High Commission, 1957.

Allen, D. G. *In English Ways.* Chapel Hill: University of North Carolina Press, 1981.

Allgemeines Landrecht für die Preussischen Staaten. 5 vols. Berlin: G. C. Nauck, 1832.

Allott, A. N. "Family Property in West Africa." In *Family Law in Asia and Africa*, edited by J. N. D. Anderson, 121–42. London: Allen & Unwin, 1968.

Anderson, Terry, and F. S. McChesney, eds. *Property Rights: Contract, Conflict, and Law.* Princeton: Princeton University Press, 2003.

Anschütz, Gerhard. "Deichwesen." In Conrad et al., *Handwörterbuch der Staatswissenschaften*, 3:462–81.

Aquinas, Thomas. "De Regno ad Regem Cypri". In *Compendium Theologiae: Opera Omnia Iussu Leonis XIII*, 42:449–71. Rome: Editori di San Tommaso, 1979.

Archives of Maryland. 72 vols. Baltimore, 1883–1972.

Archives parlementaires de 1787 à 1860. Edited by M. J. Mavidal et al. 100+ vols. Paris: Librairie Administrative de P. Dupont, 1862–.

Arndt, [...]. "Bergbau." In Conrad et al., *Handwörterbuch der Staatswissenschaften*, 2:742–54.

Arrest de la cour de parlement . . . défenses aux soi-disans Jésuites, 6 août 1762. Paris: Pierre-Guillaume Simon, 1762.

Austen, Jane, *Emma: A Novel.* London: John Murray, 1816.

Azo. *Die quaestiones des Azo.* Edited by Ernst Landsberg. Freiburg: J. C. B. Mohr, 1888.

[Bacon, Matthew]. *A New Abridgement of the Law.* 6 vols. London: E. and R. Nutt, and R. Gosling, for H. Lintot, 1736–66.

Bailyn, Bernard. *Ideological Origins of the American Revolution*. 2nd ed. Cambridge, Mass.: Harvard University Press, 1992.
Baker, K. M. "Political Languages of the French Revolution." In *Cambridge History of Eighteenth Century Political Thought*, edited by M. Goldie and R. Wokler, 626–59. Cambridge: Cambridge University Press, 2006.
Baker, Philip, ed. *The Putney Debates: The Levellers*. London: Verso, 2007.
Baldus de Ubaldis. *In Usus Feudorum Commentaria*. In *Opus Aureum Utriusque Iuris Luminis*. Lyon: Joannes Pidierius, 1550.
Balestracci, Duccio. "La politica delle acque urbane nell'Italia comunale." *Mélanges de l'École française de Rome* 104 (1992): *Moyen âge*: 431–79.
Ballard, A., and J. Tait, eds. *British Borough Charters, 1216–1307*. Cambridge: Cambridge University Press, 1923.
Baltl, Hermann, and Gernot Rocher. *Österreichische Rechtsgeschichte*. 10th ed. Graz: Leykam, 2004.
Bankton, Andrew McDouall, Lord. *An Institute of the Laws of Scotland*. Edinburgh: Stair Society, nos. 41–43, 1993–95.
Banner, Stuart. *How the Indians Lost Their Land: Law and Power on the Frontier*. Cambridge, Mass.: Belknap, 2005.
Barber, Malcolm. *The Trial of the Templars*. Cambridge: Cambridge University Press, 1978.
Barckhausen, H., ed. *Livre des coutumes*. Bordeaux: Archives Municipales, 1890.
Bardonnet, A., ed. "Comptes et enquêtes d'Alphonse comte de Poitou." In *Archives historiques du Poitou*, no. 8, 39–56. Poitiers: Société des archives historiques du Poitou, 1879.
Barnard, F. M. "National Culture and Political Legitimacy: Herder and Rousseau." *Journal of the History of Ideas* 44 (1983): 231–53.
Barnwell, P. S., and M. Mostert, eds. *Political Assemblies in the Earlier Middle Ages*. Turnhout: Brepols, 2003.
Baroni, M. F., ed. *Atti del comune di Milano nel secolo XIII*. 2 vols. Milan: Alessandria, 1976.
Bartolus of Sassoferrato. *Opera*. 5 vols. Basel: Ex officina Episcopiana, 1588–89.
Barton, John, and John Muddiman. *The Oxford Bible Commentary*. Oxford: Oxford University Press, 2001.
Bates, David, ed. *Regesta Regum Anglo-Normannorum: Acta of William I*. Oxford: Clarendon Press, 1998.

Bay, Elihu Hall. *Reports of Cases Argued and Determined in the Superior Courts of Law in the State of South Carolina since the Revolution.* 2 vols. New York: I. Riley, 1811.

Beaumanoir, Philippe de Remi, Sire de. *Coutumes de Beauvaisis.* Edited by A. Salmon. 3 vols. Paris: A. Picard, 1900.

Beautemps-Beaupré, C. J., ed. *Coutumes et institutions de l'Anjou et du Maine: Première partie: Coutumes et styles.* Paris: A. Durand et Pedone-Lauriel, 1877–83.

Becker, Lawrence C. *Property Rights: Philosophical Foundations.* London: Routledge and Kegan Paul, 1977.

Bennett, T. W. "Terminology and Land Tenure in Customary Law: An Exercise in Linguistic Theory." *Acta Juridica 1985*, 173–87. Cape Town: Juta and Co., 1986.

Bentham, Jeremy. *The Theory of Legislation.* Edited by C. K. Ogden. London: K. Paul, Trench, Trubner, 1931.

Berend, Nora. *At the Gate of Christendom: Jews, Muslims and "Pagans" in Medieval Hungary.* Cambridge: Cambridge University Press, 2001.

Betto, Bianca, ed. *Statuti del comune di Treviso.* FSI no. 109. Rome: Istituto Storico Italiano, 1984.

Beugnot, A. A., ed. *Les Olim.* 3 vols. in 4. Paris: Imprimerie Royale, 1839–48.

Birks, P. B. H. "The Roman Law Concept of Dominium and the Idea of Absolute Ownership." *Acta Juridica 1985*, 1–37. Cape Town: Juta and Co., 1986.

Blackstone, William. *Commentaries on the Laws of England.* 5th ed. 4 vols. Oxford: Clarendon Press, 1773.

Blake, E. O., ed. *Liber Eliensis.* Camden 4th Ser., vol. 92. London: Royal Historical Society, 1962.

Boas, George. *Primitivism and Related Ideas in the Middle Ages.* 2nd ed. Baltimore: Johns Hopkins University Press, 1997.

Bobbio, Norberto. *Thomas Hobbes and the Natural Law Tradition.* Translated by D. Gobetti. Chicago: University of Chicago Press, 1993.

Bocchi, Francesca. *Atlante storico delle città italiane: Bologna.* 3 vols. Bologna: Grafis Edizioni, 1995–96.

Bohannan, Paul, and Laura Bohannan. *Tiv Economy.* Evanston: Northwestern University Press, 1968.

Bonaini, F., ed. *Statuti inediti della città di Pisa.* 2 vols. Florence: Presso G. P. Vieusseux, 1854–70.

Borelli, G. B., ed. *Editti antichi e nuovi de' sovrani prencipi della real casa di Savoia*. Turin: Bartolomeo Zappata, 1681.
Borrelli de Serres, L. L. "L'agrandissement du palais de la Cité sous Philippe-le-Bel." *Mémoires de la société de l'histoire de Paris et de l'Ile de France* 38(1911): 1–106.
Bosio, Casimiro de'. *Della espropriazione e degli altri danni che si recano per causa di pubblica*. 2 vols. Venice: Pietro Naratovich, 1856–57.
Brett, Annabel. *Liberty, Right and Nature*. Cambridge: Cambridge University Press, 1997.
Buc, Philippe. *L'ambiguité du livre: Prince, pouvoir et peuple dans les commentaires de la Bible au moyen âge*. Paris: Beauchesne, 1994.
Buckle, Stephen. *Natural Law and the Theory of Property*. Oxford: Clarendon Press, 1991.
Burke, Edmund, *Reflections on the Revolution in France*. Edited by C. C. O'Brien. Harmondsworth: Penguin Books, 1968.
Burlamaqui, Jean-Jacques. *Principes du droit naturel et politique*. 3 vols. Geneva: Cl. & Ant. Philibert, 1764.
———. *Principles of Natural and Politic Law*. Translated by Mr. Nugent. 2 vols. London: Nourse, 1763.
Burns, J. H., ed. *Cambridge History of Medieval Political Thought*. Cambridge: Cambridge University Press, 1988.
Bush, Bernard, ed. *Laws of the Royal Colony of New Jersey*. 5 vols. Trenton: New Jersey State Library, Archives and History Bureau, 1977–86.
Bynkershoek, Cornelius van. *Quaestionum Juris Publici Libri Duo*. Leiden: Joannes van Kerckhem, 1737.
Calendar of Inquisitions Miscellaneous. 8 vols. London: HMSO, 1916–2003.
Calendar of the Charter Rolls. 6 vols. London: HMSO, 1903–20.
Calendar of the Close Rolls. 47 vols. London: HMSO, 1892–1963.
Calendar of the Liberate Rolls. 6 vols. London: HMSO, 1916–64.
Calendar of the Patent Rolls. 22 vols., London: HMSO, 1897–1986.
Campi, Pietro Maria. *Dell'historia ecclesiastica di Piacenza*. 3 vols. Piacenza: Giovanni Bazachi, 1651–62.
Canning, Joseph. "The Corporation in the Political Thought of the Italian Jurists of the Thirteenth and Fourteenth Centuries." *History of Political Thought* 1 (1980): 9–32.
———. *The Political Thought of Baldus de Ubaldis*. Cambridge: Cambridge University Press, 1987.

Capitularia Regum Francorum. Edited by A. Boretius. 2 vols. MGH Legum Sectio 2. Hanover: Hahn, 1883–1901.

Cárdenas, Francisco de. *Ensayo sobre la historia de la propiedad territorial en España*. 2 vols. Madrid: J. Noguera, á cargo de M. Martinez, 1873.

Carlyle, A. J. "Some Aspects of the Relation of Roman Law to Political Principles in the Middle Ages." In *Studi di storia e diritto in onore di Enrico Besta*, 3:185–98. Milan: Giuffre, 1939.

Carlyle, R. W., and A. J. Carlyle. *A History of Mediaeval Political Theory in the West*. 6 vols. Edinburgh: W. Blackwood, 1962.

Carolus-Barré, L. *Le procès de canonisation de Saint Louis*. Rome: École française de Rome, 1899.

Caruana Gomez de Barreda, Jaime, ed. *Fuero latino de Teruel*. Teruel: Instituto de Estudios Turolenses, 1974.

Cheshire, G. C. *The Modern Law of Real Property*. London: Butterworth, 1925.

Cheyette, Fredric L. "La justice et le pouvoir royal à la fin du moyen âge français." *Revue historique de droit français et étranger*, 4th ser., 40 (1962): 373–94.

Chinhengo, A. M. "Expropriation in Zimbabwe, 1890–1995." In *L'expropriation*, RSJB 67 (2000): 351–95.

Christianson, Paul. "Political Thought in Early Stuart England." *Historical Journal* 30 (1987): 955–70.

Chronica monasterii de Melsa. Edited by E. A. Bond. Rolls Series no. 98. 3 vols. London: Longmans, Green, Reader, and Dyer, 1866–68.

Cilleuls, Alfred des. *Origines et développement du régime des travaux publics en France*. Paris: Imprimerie nationale, 1895.

Cipolla. C., ed. *Codice Diplomatico del monastero di S. Colombano di Bobbio*. 3 vols. FSI nos. 52–54. Rome: Istituto Storico Italiano, 1918.

Clifford, Frederick. *A History of Private Bill Legislation*. 2 vols. London: Butterworth, 1885–87.

Cogan, Neil H., ed. *The Complete Bill of Rights*. New York: Oxford University Press, 1997.

Colvin, H. M., ed. *The History of the King's Works*. 6 vols. London: HMSO, 1963–82.

Concilia Aevi Karolini. Edited by A. Werminghoff. MGH Concilia, 2 (1). Hanover: Hahn, 1906.

Conrad, Hermann. *Deutsche Rechtsgeschichte*. 2 vols. Karlsruhe: Müller, 1954, 1966.

Conrad, J., et al., eds. *Handwörterbuch der Staatswissenschaften*. 8 vols. Jena: G. Fischer, 1909–11.
Constitutiones dominii Mediolanensis. Milan: Vincentius Meda, 1541.
Constitutiones et Acta Publica Imperatorum et Regum. 11 vols. MGH Legum Sectio 4. Hanover/Weimar: Hahn/Bühlaus, 1893–1992.
Constitutiones y leyes fundamentales de España (1808–1947). Edited by A. Padilla Serra. Granada, 1954.
Cooper, Edward. *Castillos señoriales en la corona de Castilla*. 3 vols. in 4. Valladolid: Junta de Castilla y León, Consejería de Cultura y Turismo, 1991.
Cortes de los antiguos reinos de Aragon y de Valencia y principado de Cataluña: Cortes de Cataluña. 26 vols. Madrid: Real Academia de la Historia, 1896–1922.
Cortes de los antiguos reinos de Leon y de Castilla. 5 vols. Madrid: Real Academia de la Historia, 1861–1903.
Cortese, Ennio. *La norma giuridica*. 2 vols. Milan: Giuffrè, 1962–64.
Cripps, C. A. *Treatise on the Principles of the Law of Compensation in Reference to the Land Clauses Consolidation Acts*. London: Sweet, 1881.
Crouzet-Pavan, Élisabeth. "'Pour le bien commun.' A propos des politiques urbaines dans l'Italie communale." In *Pouvoir et édilité: Les grands chantiers dans l'Italie communale et seigneuriale*, edited by E. Crouzet-Pavan, 11–40. Rome: École française de Rome, 2003.
Cunningham, Roger A., William B. Stoebuck, and D. A. Whitman. *The Law of Property*. St. Paul: West, 1993.
Cushing, John D., ed. *Laws and Liberties of Massachusetts*. 3 vols. Wilmington, Del.: Scholarly Resources, 1976.
Dagger, Richard. "Rights." In *Political Innovation and Conceptual Change*, edited by Terence Ball et al., 292–308. Cambridge: Cambridge University Press, 1989.
Dallas, A. J., *Reports of Cases Ruled and Adjudged in the Several Courts of the United States and of Pennsylvania*. 3 vols. Philadelphia: Aurora Office, 1798–1807.
Danzer, M., ed. *Bayerische Landrecht, Codex Maximilianeus Bavaricus Civilis, vom Jahre 1756 in seinen heutigen Geltung*. Munich: J. Schweizer Verlag, 1894.
Dareste, Rodolphe, and Pierre Dareste. *La justice administrative en France*. 2nd ed. Paris: Librairie de la société du recueil général des lois et des arrêts, 1898.

Davies, Wendy. *Acts of Giving: Individual, Community, and Church in Tenth-Century Christian Spain*. Oxford: Oxford University Press, 2007.

Davies, Wendy, and Paul Fouracre, eds. *Settlement of Disputes in Early Medieval Europe*. Cambridge: Cambridge University Press, 1986.

Deedes, Cecil, ed. *Registrum Johannis de Pontissara*. 2 vols. London: Canterbury and York Society, 1915–24.

Delaborde, H. F., et al., eds. *Recueil des actes de Philippe Auguste*. 6 vols. Paris: Imprimerie nationale, 1916–2005.

Diderot, Denis, and J. le Rond d'Alembert. *Encyclopédie*. 17 vols. Paris: Brasson et al., 1751–65.

Diplomata Regum et Imperatorum Germaniae. 18 vols. MGH Diplomata, 1879–2006.

Domat, Jean. *Les loix civiles dans leur ordre naturel, le droit public et legum delectus*. 2nd ed. 2 vols. Paris: Guillaume Cavelier, 1705.

Domesday Book. Edited by H. Ellis. 4 vols. London: Record Commission, 1783, 1816.

Donahue, Charles. "The Future of the Concept of Property Predicted from Its Past." *Nomos* 22 (1980): 28–68.

Duchesne, L., ed. *Liber Pontificalis*. 2 vols. Paris: Ernest Thorin, 1886–92.

Du Moulin, Charles. *Prima Pars Commentariorum in Consuetudines Parisienses: De Feudis*. In *Opera*, vol. 1. Paris: Antonius Dezallier, 1681.

Dumville, David. *Wessex and England from Alfred to Edgar*. Woodbridge: Boydell Press, 1992.

Dunbabin, Jean. "Government." In Burns, *Cambridge History of Medieval Political Thought*, 477–519.

Dussaix, Caroline. "Les moulins à Reggio d'Emilia aux xiie et xiiie siècles." *Mélanges de l'École française de Rome* 91 (1979): *Moyen âge, temps modernes*: 113–47.

Dussert, Auguste. *Essai historique sur La Mure*. 2nd ed. Paris: Alphonse Picard & Fils, 1903.

Eisenhardt, Ulrich. *Deutsche Rechtsgeschichte*. Munich: C. H. Beck, 1984.

Elenchus fontium historiae urbanae. Edited by C. van de Kieft et al. 4 vols. Leiden: E. J. Brill, 1967–96.

Ellickson, Robert C. "Property in Land." *Yale Law Journal* 102 (1993): 1315–1400.

Ely, James W. "'That Due Satisfaction Be Made': The Fifth Amendment and the Origins of the Compensation Principle." *AJLH* 36 (1992): 1–18.

Epistolae Bonifatii et Lullii. Edited by M. Tangl. MGH Epistolae Selectae 1. Berlin: Weidmannsche Verlagsbuchhandlung, 1916.

Epstein, Richard A. *Takings: Private Property and the Power of Eminent Domain*. Cambridge Mass.: Harvard University Press, 1985.

Erler, A., and E. Kaufmann, eds. *Handwörterbuch zur deutschen Rechtsgeschichte*. 5 vols. Berlin: E. Schmidt, 1964–98.

Erskine, John. *An Institute of the Law of Scotland*. Edited by A. Macallan. 2 vols. Edinburgh: Edinburgh Printing and Publishing Co., 1838. Originally published in 1773.

Escobar, Jesús R. *The Plaza Mayor and the Shaping of Baroque Madrid*. Cambridge: Cambridge University Press, 2003.

Esmein, A. *Cours élémentaire d'histoire du droit français*. 2nd. ed. Paris: Librairie de Recueil, 1895.

Espinas, Georges, ed. *Privilèges et chartes de franchises de la Flandre*. 2 vols. Brussels: Commission royale des anciennes lois et ordonnances de Belgique, 1959–61.

Établissements de Saint Louis. Edited by Paul Viollet. 4 vols. Paris: Renouard, 1881–86.

Faith, Rosamond. *The English Peasantry and the Growth of Lordship*. London: Leicester University Press, 1997.

Falcone, E., and R. Peveri, eds. *Il registrum magnum del comune di Piacenza*. 5 vols. Milan: A. Giuffrè, 1984–97.

Fasoli, G., and P. Sella, eds. *Statuti di Bologna dell' anno 1288*. 2 vols. Vatican City: Biblioteca apostolica vaticana Rome, 1939.

Fauré, Christine, ed. *Déclarations de droits de l'homme de 1789*. Paris: Payot, 1988.

Feenstra, Robert. "Der Eigentumsbegriff bei Hugo Grotius im Licht einiger mittelalterlicher und spätscholastischer Quellen." In *Festschrift für F. Wieacker*, edited by O. Behrends et al., 209–34. Göttingen: Vandenhoeck und Ruprecht, 1978.

———. "Dominium utile est chimaera: Nouvelles réflexions sur le concept de propriété dans le droit savant." *Revue d'histoire du droit* 66 (1998): 381–97.

———. "Expropriation et *dominium eminens* chez Grotius." In *L'expropriation*, RSJB 66 (1999): 133–53.

———. "Les origines du dominium utile chez les glossateurs." In *Flores Legum H. J. Scheltema ... Oblati*, 49–93. Groningen: Wolters-Noordhoff, 1971.

Fernández-Santamaria, J. A. *The State, War and Peace: Spanish Political Thought in the Renaissance, 1516–1559.* Cambridge: Cambridge University Press, 1977.

Finn, R. Welldon. "Hampshire." In *The Domesday Geography of South-East England*, edited by H. C. Darby and E. M. J. Campbell, 287–363. Cambridge: Cambridge University Press, 1962.

Finnis, John. *Aquinas: Moral, Political, and Legal Theory.* Oxford: Oxford University Press, 1998.

Firth, Raymond. *Primitive Polynesian Economy.* 2nd ed. London: Routledge & Kegan Paul, 1965.

Fleming, Robin. *Domesday Book and the Law.* Cambridge: Cambridge University Press, 1998.

Ford, W. C., et al., eds. *Journals of the Continental Congress, 1774–1783.* 34 vols. Washington: U.S. Government Printing Office, 1904–37.

Fossier, Robert. *La Terre et les hommes en Picardie.* Paris: Béatrice-Nauwelaerts, 1968.

Fouracre, Paul. *The Age of Charles Martel.* Harlow: Longman, 2000.

———. "Carolingian Justice: The Rhetoric of Improvement and Contexts of Abuse." *Settimane di studio del centro italiano di studi sull'alto medioevo* 42 (1995): 771–803.

———. "Cultural Conformity in Early Medieval Europe." *History Workshop* 33 (1992): 152–61.

Franklin, Benjamin. "Queries and Remarks respecting Alterations in the Constitution of Pennsylvania." In *Writings*, edited by A. H. Smyth, 10:54–60. New York: Macmillan, 1907.

Fratri, L., ed. *Statuti di Bologna dell'anno 1245 all'anno 1267.* 3 vols. Bologna: Regia Tipografia, 1869–77.

Freedman, Paul. *Images of the Medieval Peasant.* Stanford: Stanford University Press, 1999.

Fried, Johannes. "*Gens* und *Regnum*. Wahrnehmuungs- und Deutungs Kategorien politischen Wandels im früheren Mittelalter. Bemerkungen zur doppelten Theoriebindung des Historikers." In *Sozialer Wandel im Mittelalter*, edited by Jürgen Miethke and Klaus Schreiner, 73–104. Sigmaringen: J. Thorbecke, 1994.

Friedberg, A., ed. *Corpus Iuris Canonici.* 2nd ed. 2 vols. Graz: Academische Druck, 1955.

Friedman, Lawrence M. *History of American Law.* New York: Simon & Schuster, 1985.

Frier, Bruce W. *Landlord and Tenant in Imperial Rome*. Princeton: Princeton University Press, 1980.

Garcia Espuche, Albert, et al. "Barcelona." In *Atlas histórico de ciudades europeas: Península Ibérica*, edited by Manuel Guardia et al., 63–94. Barcelona: Salvat Editores, 1994.

Gatta, F. S., ed. *Liber grossus antiquus comunis Regii*. 6 vols. Reggio Emilia: U. Costi, 1944–62.

Gaudemet, Jean. "*Utilitas Publica*." *Revue historique de droit français et étranger*, 4th ser., 29 (1951): 465–99.

Ghoshal, Upendranatha. *Agrarian System in Ancient India*. Calcutta: University of Calcutta, 1930.

Gierke, Otto. *Deutsches Privatrecht*. 2 vols. Leipzig: Duncker & Humblot, 1895, 1905.

[Gilbert, Jeffrey.] *An Historical View of the Court of Exchequer*. London: E. and R. Nutt, and R. Gosling for T. Waller, 1738.

Ginson, S., and B. Ward-Perkins. "The Surviving Remains of the Leonine Wall." *Papers of the British School at Rome* 47 (1979): 30–57; 51 (1983): 222–39.

Gislain, Geoffroy de. 'L'expropriation en France au moyen âge.' In *Orlandis 70: Estudios de drecho y penal romano feudal*, 174–86. Barcelona: PPU, 1988.

Gluckman, Max. *The Ideas in Barotse Jurisprudence*. 2nd. ed. Manchester: Manchester University Press, 1972.

———. *The Judicial Process among the Barotse of Northern Rhodesia*. Manchester: Manchester University Press, 1955.

Goebel, Julius. "Courts and the Law in Colonial New York." In *Essays in the History of Early American Law*, 245–77. Chapel Hill: University of North Carolina Press, 1969.

———. "King's Law and Local Custom." In *Essays in the History of Early American Law*, 83–120. Chapel Hill: University of North Carolina Press, 1969.

Goetz, Hans-Werner. "Perceptions of 'Power' and 'State' in the Early Middle Ages: The Case of the Astronomer's Life of Louis the Pious." In *Representations of Power in Medieval Germany, 800–1500*, edited by Björn Weiler and Simon Maclean, 15–36. Turnhout: Brepols, 2006.

———. "Regnum: Zum politischen Denken der Karolingerzeit." *Zeitschrift der Savigny-Stiftung für Rechtsgeschichte, Germ. Abteilung* 104 (1987): 110–89.

Goffart, Walter. *The Le Mans Forgeries.* Cambridge, Mass.: Harvard University Press, 1966.
Gonzales, Julio, ed. *Regesta de Fernando II.* Madrid: Consejo Superior de Investigaciones Científicas, 1943.
Gordon, Robert W. "Paradoxical Property." In *Early Modern Conceptions of Property,* edited by John Brewer and S. Staves, 95–110. London: Routledge, 1995.
Gorosch, Max, ed. *Fuero de Teruel.* Stockholm: Almqvist & Wiksells, 1950.
Grant, J. A. C. "The 'Higher Law' Background of the Law of Eminent Domain." *Wisconsin Law Review* 6 (1931): 67–85.
Greene, Jack P. *All Men Are Created Equal: Some Reflections on the Character of the American Revolution.* Oxford: Clarendon Press, 1976.
Griswold, C. L. "Rights and Wrongs." In *A Culture of Rights,* edited by M. J. Lacey and K. Haakonssen, 144–214. Cambridge: Cambridge University Press, 1993.
Gross, Jean-Pierre. *Fair Shares for All: Jacobin Egalitarianism in Practice.* Cambridge: Cambridge University Press, 1997.
Grotius, Hugo [Hugo de Groot]. *De Iure Belli ac Pacis Libri Tres.* Paris: Nicolaus Buon, 1625.
———. *Inleidinge tot de Hollandsche Rechtsgeleerdheid.* Edited by F. Dovring et al. Leiden: Universitaire Pers, 1952.
Guillaume le Breton. *Gesta Philippi Augusti.* In *Oeuvres de Rigord et de Guillaume le Breton,* edited by H. F. Delaborde, 1:168–333. Paris: Renouard, 1882–85.
Haakonssen, Knud. *Natural Law and Moral Philosophy: From Grotius to the Scottish Enlightenment.* Cambridge: Cambridge University Press, 1996.
Haase, Carl. "Die mittelalterliche Stadt als Festung." In *Die Stadt des Mittelalters,* 1:377–407. Darmstadt: Wissenschaftliche Buchgesellschaft, 1969.
Hargrave, Francis. *Collection of Tracts relative to the Law of England.* London: T. Wright, 1787.
Harouel, Jean-Louis. *Histoire de l'expropriation.* Paris: Presses Universitaires de France, 2000.
———. *L'embellissement des villes: L'urbanisme français au xviiie siècle.* Paris: Picard, 1993.
———. "L'expropriation dans l'histoire du droit français." In *L'expropriation,* RSJB 67 (2000): 39–77.

Harris, James W., "Reason or Mumbo Jumbo: The Common Law's Approach to Property." *Proceedings of the British Academy* 117 (2002): 445–75.

Harris, Marshall. *Origin of the Land Tenure System in the United States.* Ames: Iowa State College Press, 1953.

Harris, M. D., ed. *Coventry Leet Book.* 2 vols. London: Oxford University Press for Early English Text Society, 1907–13.

Hart, John F. "Expropriation in America before 1776: Preliminary Observations." In *L'expropriation*, RSJB 67 (2000): 335–43.

———. "Taking and Compensation in Early America." *AJLH* 40 (1996): 253–305.

Hecht, Neil. "From Seisin to Sit-in: Evolving Property Concepts." *Boston University Law Review* 44 (1964): 435–66.

Heers, Jacques. "En Italie centrale: Les paysages construits." In *D'une ville à l'autre*, 279–322. Rome: École française de Rome, 1989.

———. "Porta aurea à Genes: Bourg de réligieux, bourg d'immigrés." In *Fortifications, portes de villes, places publiques dans le monde méditerranéen*, edited by J. Heers, 255–76. Paris: Université de Paris-Sorbonne, 1985.

Heineccius, J. G. *Elementa Juris Naturae et Gentium.* Halle: Orphanotropheum, 1738.

Hening, W. M., ed. *Statutes at Large . . . of Virginia . . . from 1619.* 13 vols. New York, 1819–23. Reprinted, Charlottesville: University Press of Virginia, 1969.

Henry of Huntingdon. *Historia Anglorum.* Edited by D. Greenway. Oxford: Oxford University Press, 1996.

Herr, Richard. *Rural Change and Royal Finances in Spain at the End of the Old Regime.* Berkeley: University of California Press, 1989.

Hibst, Peter. *Utilitas Publica-Gemeiner Nutz-Gemeinwohl.* Frankfurt: Lang, 1991.

Hill, David. "The Burghal Hidage." *Medieval Archaeology* 13 (1969): 84–92.

Hoadly, Charles J., ed. *Public Records of the Colony of Connecticut, 1689–1706.* Hartford, 1868.

Hobbes, Thomas. *Leviathan.* Edited by Richard Tuck. Cambridge: Cambridge University Press, 1996.

Holdsworth, W. S. *History of English Law.* 17 vols. London: Methuen, 1922–72.

Holt, J. C. *Magna Carta*. Cambridge: Cambridge University Press, 1965.
Holtz, [...]. "Krieg und Enteignung in der Mark vor 300 Jahren." *Deutsche Juristen-Zeitung* 23 (1918): 287–91.
Honoré, A. M. "Ownership." In *Oxford Essays in Jurisprudence*, edited by A. G. Guest, 107–47. Oxford: Oxford University Press, 1961.
Hooker, Richard. *Ecclesiastical Polity*. Edited by Isaac Walton. 2 vols. Oxford: Clarendon Press, 1890.
Horne, Thomas A. *Property Rights and Poverty: Political Argument in Britain 1605–1834*. Chapel Hill: University of North Carolina Press, 1990.
Horwitz, Morton. *The Transformation of American Law*. Cambridge, Mass.: Harvard University Press, 1977. Reprinted, New York: Oxford University Press, 1992.
Hubert, H. W. *Der Palazzo comunale von Bologna*. Cologne: Böhlau, 1993.
Hudson, Tim. "The Origins of Steyning and Bramber, Sussex." *Southern History* 2 (1980): 11–29.
Hutson, James H. "The Bill of Rights and the American Revolutionary Experience." In *A Culture of Rights*, edited by M. J. Lacey and K. Haakonssen, 62–97. Cambridge: Cambridge University Press, 1993.
Inderwick, F. A. *The Story of King Edward and New Winchelsea*. London: Sampson Low & Co., 1892.
Innes, Matthew. *State and Society in the Early Middle Ages*. Cambridge: Cambridge University Press, 2000.
Isambert, F. A., et al., eds. *Recueil général des anciennes lois françaises*. 29 vols. Paris: Belin-Le-Prieur, 1822–33.
Jefferson, Thomas. *Papers*. Edited by J. P. Boyd et al. 27 vols. Princeton: Princeton University Press, 1950–97.
Jeserich, Kurt G. A., et al. *Deutsche Verwaltungsgeschichte*. 6 vols. Stuttgart: Deutsche Verlags-Anstalt, 1983–88.
Jones, J. Walter. "Expropriation in Roman Law." *Law Quarterly Review* 45 (1929): 512–27.
Jordan, William C. *The French Monarchy and the Jews*. Philadelphia: University of Pennsylvania Press, 1989.
Journal of the House of Delegates of the Commonwealth of Virginia. Richmond, 1828. (Library of Congress microfiche.)
Justi, J. H. G. von. *Staatswirthschaft oder systematische Abhandlung aller Oeconomischen und Cameral-Wissenschaftern die sur Regierung eines*

Landes erfordert werden. 2nd. ed. 2 vols. Leipzig: Bernhard Christoph Breitkopf, 1758.

Karabélias, Evangélos. "L'expropriation en droit grec ancien." In *L'expropriation*, RSJB 66 (1999): 21–54.

Kayser, C. G. *Vollständiges Bücher-Lexicon.* 42 vols. Leipzig: Ludwig Schumann, 1834–1912.

Keane, John. *Tom Paine: A Political Life.* London: Bloomsbury, 1995.

Kempshall, Martin. *The Common Good in Late Medieval Political Thought.* Oxford: Clarendon Press, 1999.

King, P. D. "The Barbarian Kingdoms." In Burns, *Cambridge History of Medieval Political Thought*, 123–41.

Kosambi, Damodar D. "Origins of Feudalism in Kashmir." In *Feudal Social Formation in Early India*, edited by Dwijendra N. Jha, 130–44. Delhi: Chanakya, 1987.

Kroeschell, Karl. *Deutsche Rechtsgeschichte.* 2 vols. Opladen: Westdeutscher Verlag, 1980.

Kutler, Stanley I., ed. *Dictionary of American History.* 3rd ed. 10 vols. New York: Scribner, 2003.

Lalande, Joseph Jérôme le Français de. *Des canaux de navigation et spécialement du canal de Languedoc.* Paris: Veuve Desaint, 1778.

La Mare, Nicolas de. *Traité de la police.* 4 vols. Paris: J. & P. Cot, 1705–38; vol. 4 by La Cler du Brillet.

Lambert, Sheila. *Bills and Acts: Legislative Procedures in Eighteenth-Century England.* Cambridge: Cambridge University Press, 1971.

Landrecht, Policey: Gerichts-, Malefitz- vnd andere Ordnungen. Der Fürstenthumben Obern vnd Nidern Bayrn. Munich: Nicolaus Henricus, 1616.

Las Casas, Bartolomé de. *De Regia Potestate.* Edited by L. Perena et al. Madrid: Consejo Superior de Investigaciones Científicas, 1969.

———. *Los tesoros de Peru.* Edited by A. Losada. Madrid: Consejo Superior de Investigaciones Científicas, 1958.

Layer, Max. *Principien des Enteignungsrecht.* Leipzig: Duncker & Humblot, 1902.

Lehmann, Carl, ed. *Das Langobardische Lehnrecht.* Göttingen: Dieterich, 1896. Reprinted in *Consuetudines Feudorum*, edited by K. A. Eckhardt. Aalen: Scientia Verlag, 1971.

Lenhoff, Arthur. "Development of the Concept of Eminent Domain." *Columbia Law Review* 42 (1942): 596–638.

León Tello, Pilar. *Judíos de Toledo*. 2 vols. Madrid: Consejo Superior de Investigaciones Científicas, 1979.

Leroy, Maxime. *Histoire des idées sociales en France*. 3 vols. Paris: Gallimard, 1946–54.

Lesne, Émile. *Histoire de la propriété ecclésiastique en France*. 6 vols. Lille: R. Giard; Paris: H. Champion, 1910–43.

Levy, Leonard W. *Origins of the Bill of Rights*. New Haven: Yale University Press, 1999.

Lewis, J. *A Treatise on the Law of Eminent Domain*. 3rd ed. 2 vols. Chicago: Callaghan, 1909.

L'expropriation. 2 vols. RSJB 66 and 67. Brussels: De Boeck Université, 1999–2000.

Leyte, Guillaume. *Domaine et domanialité publique dans la France médiévale (xiie–xve)*. Strasbourg: Presses Universitaires de Strasbourg, 1996.

Liber Iurium Reipublicae Genuensis. 2 vols. Monumenta Historiae Patriae, nos. 7, 8. Turin: Fratres Bocca, 1854, 1857.

Lieberman, David. "Property, Commerce, and the Common Law." In *Early Modern Conceptions of Property*, edited by John Brewer and S. Staves, 144–58. London: Routledge, 1995.

Lincoln, Charles Z., et al., eds. *Colonial Laws of New York*. 5 vols. Albany: J. B. Lyon, 1894.

Livesey, James. *Making Democracy in the French Revolution*. Cambridge, Mass.: Harvard University Press, 2001.

Locke, John. *Two Treatises of Government*. Edited by P. Laslett. Cambridge: Cambridge University Press, 1967.

Loersch, H., and R. Schroeder, eds. *Urkunden zur Geschichte des deutschen Privatrechtes*. Bonn: B. A. Marcus, 1874.

López, Gregorio, ed. *Siete partidas*. Facsimile of 1555 ed., published in Salamanca. 7 vols. in 3. Madrid: Boletín Oficial del Estado, 1985.

Louis XIV. *Mémoires de Louis XIV pour l'instruction du Dauphin*. Edited by Charles L. Dreyss. 2 vols. Paris: Didier, 1860.

Lovejoy, Arthur O., and G. Boas. *Primitivism and Related Ideas in Antiquity*. Baltimore: Johns Hopkins University Press, 1997.

Lozano Corbi, Enrique. "¿Existió en la epoca republicana romana el derecho a la expropiación forzoza por causa de utilidad pública?" In *L'expropriation*, RSJB 66 (1999): 115–22.

Lucas, Paul. "*Ex parte* Sir William Blackstone, Plagiarist: A Note on Blackstone and the Natural Law." *AJLH* 7 (1968): 142–58.

[Lulius, D., et al.]. *Rechtsgeleerde Observatien . . . uyt De Inleidinge tot de Hollandsche Rechtsgel. van Mr Hugo de Groot*. The Hague: Johannes Mensert, 1777.

Machen, A. W. "Corporate Personality." *Harvard Law Review* 24 (1911): 253–67, 347–65.

Mair, Lucy. *Introduction to Social Anthropology*. Oxford: Clarendon Press, 1965.

Maistre, André. *Le canal des deux mers: Canal royal du Languedoc, 1666–1810*. Toulouse: Édouard Privat, 1968.

Maitland, F. W. *Constitutional History of England*. Cambridge: Cambridge University Press, 1908. Reprinted, 1946.

———. *The Letters of Frederic William Maitland*. Edited by C. H. S. Fifoot. Selden Society, Supplementary Series, no. 1. London: Selden Society, 1965.

———, ed. *Memoranda de Parliamento*. Rolls Series no. 98. London: HMSO, 1893.

Maitland, F. W., et al., eds. *Eyre of Kent, 1313–1314*. Selden Society, vol. 24. London: Selden Society, 1909.

Malcolm, Noel. *Aspects of Hobbes*. Oxford: Clarendon Press, 2002.

Malet, Hugh. *Bridgewater: The Canal Duke*. Nelson, Eng.: Hendon, 1990.

Manaresi, C., ed. *Atti del comune di Milano fino all'anno MCCXVI*. Milan: Capriolo & Massimino, 1919.

Mandelli, Vittorio. *Il comune di Vercelli nel medioevo*. 4 vols. Vercelli: Guglielmoni, 1857–61.

Mann, P. A. "Outlines of a History of Expropriation." *Law Quarterly Review* 75 (1959): 188–219.

Markus, W. A. "The Latin Fathers." In Burns, *Cambridge History of Medieval Political Thought*, 92–122.

Mason, J. F. A. "The Rapes of Sussex and the Norman Conquest." *Sussex Archaeological Collections* 102 (1964): 68–93.

Matthews, Nathan. "The Valuation of Property in the Roman Law." *Harvard Law Review* 34 (1921): 229–59.

Mayer, David N. *The Constitutional Thought of Thomas Jefferson*. Charlottesville: University Press of Virginia, 1994.

Mayr, G. K., ed. *Sammlung der Churpfalz-Baierischen . . . Landes-Verordnungen*. 5 vols. Munich: A. M. Bitterin/Franz Hübschmann, 1784–97.

McDonald, Forrest. *Novus Ordo Seclorum: The Intellectual Origins of the Constitution.* Lawrence: University Press of Kansas, 1985.

McGovern, John. "Private Property and the Jurists, AD 1200–1500." In *In Iure Veritas: Studies in Canon Law in Memory of Schafer Williams*, edited by Steven B. Bowman and B. E. Cody, 131–58. Cincinnati: University of Cincinnati, 1991.

McManners, John. *Church and Society in Eighteenth-Century France.* 2 vols. Oxford: Clarendon Press, 1998.

Megarry, Robert, and H. W. R. Wade. *The Law of Real Property.* London: Stevens and Sons, 1957. 4th ed. London: Stevens, 1975. 6th ed. by Charles Harpum. London: Sweet and Maxwell, 2000.

Melanchthon, Philip. *Opera.* Edited by C. G. Bretschneider and H. E. Bindseil. 28 vols. Halle/Brunswick: Schwetschke, 1834–60.

Mensch, Elizabeth V. "The Colonial Origins of Liberal Property Rights." *Buffalo Law Review* 31 (1982): 635–735.

Menski, Werner. *Hindu Law: Beyond Tradition and Modernity.* Delhi: Oxford University Press, 2003.

———. *Indian Legal Systems Past and Present.* London: University of London School of Oriental and African Studies, 1997.

Merrill, Thomas W. "Property and the Right to Exclude." *Nebraska Law Review* 77 (1998): 730–55.

Mestre, Jean-Louis. "Les origines seigneuriales de l'expropriation." *Recueil des mémoires et travaux publié par la société d'histoire du droit et des institutions des anciens pays de droit écrit* 11 (1980): 71–79.

———. "L'expropriation face à la propriété (du moyen âge au code civil)." *Droits* 1 (1985): 51–62.

———. *Un droit administrative à la fin de l'ancien régime: Le contentieux des communautés de Provence.* Paris: Librairie Generale de Droit et de Jurisprudence, 1976.

Meyer, Georg. *Das Recht der Expropriation.* Leipzig: Serig'schen Buchhandlung (E. G. Hermann), 1868.

Michaud-Quantin, Pierre. *Universitas: Expressions du mouvement communautaire dans le moyen âge latin.* Paris: J. Vrin, 1970.

Mínguez Fernández, José María, et al., eds. *Colección diplomática del monasterio de Sahagún.* 7 vols. León: Centro de Estudios e Investigación San Isidoro, 1976–99.

Mommsen, T., and P. M. Meyer, eds. *Codex Theodosianus.* 2 vols. Berlin: Weidmann, 1954.

Mommsen, T., et al., eds. *Corpus Iuris Civilis*. 6th ed. 3 vols. Berlin: Weidmann, 1954.
Montesquieu, C. de Secondat, baron de. *L'esprit des lois*. 2 vols. Geneva: Barrillot & fils, 1749.
Monumenta Historiae Patriae. 19 vols. Turin: Regium Typographeum, 1836–53.
Moore, Barrington. *Injustice*. London: Macmillan, 1978.
Morgues, Jacques, ed. *Statuts et coustumes du pays de Provence*. Aix: Estienne David, 1642.
Mozzarelli, Cesare. "'Pubblico bene' e stato all fine dell'ancien regime." *Ius* 22 (1975): 235–78.
Muldoon, James. *The Americas in the Spanish World Order*. Philadelphia: University of Pennsylvania Press, 1994.
———. *Popes, Lawyers and Infidels*. Liverpool: Liverpool University Press, 1979.
Müntz, Eugène. *Les arts à la cour des papes Innocent VIII, Alexandre VI, Pie III, 1484–1503*. 3 vols. Paris: E. Thorin, 1878–82.
Munzer, Stephen R. *A Theory of Property*. Cambridge: Cambridge University Press, 1990.
Muratori, Lodovico Antonio. *Antiquitates Italicae Medii Aevi*. 6 vols. Milan: Societas Palatina, 1738–42.
Murray, Alexander C. "From Roman to Frankish Gaul: 'Centenarii' and 'Centenae' in the Administration of the Merovingian Kingdom." *Traditio* 44 (1988): 59–100.
Musset, L., ed. *Actes de Guillaume le conquérant et de la reine Mathilde pour les abbayes caennaises*. Caen: Société des antiquaires de Normandie, 1967.
Nedelsky, Jennifer. *Private Property and the Limits of American Constitutionalism*. Chicago: University of Chicago Press, 1990.
Nékám, A. *The Personality Conception of the Legal Entity*. Cambridge, Mass.: Harvard University Press, 1938.
Nelson, Craig. *Thomas Paine*. London: Profile, 2007.
Nelson, Janet L. "England and the Continent in the Ninth Century: III, Rights and Rituals." *Transactions of the Royal Historical Society*, 6th ser., 14 (2004): 1–24.
———. "Kingship and Empire." In Burns, *Cambridge History of Medieval Political Thought*, 211–51.
———. *Politics and Ritual in Early Medieval Europe*. London: Hambledon Press, 1986.

Nelson, William E. *Americanization of the Common Law: The Impact of Change on Massachusetts Society, 1760–1830*. Cambridge, Mass.: Harvard University Press, 1975.

Neusser, G. "Enteignung." In Erler and Kaufmann, *Handwörterbuch zur deutschen Rechtsgeschichte*, 1:941–44.

New, C. W. *History of the Alien Priories in England to the Confiscation of Henry V*. Chicago: Privately printed, 1916.

Nicolini, Ugo. *La proprietà, il principe e l'espropriazione per pubblica utilità: Studi sulla dottrina giuridica intermedia*. Milan: Giuffrè, 1952.

———. *Le limitazioni alla proprietà negli statuti italiani*. Mantua: Tip. industriale mantovana, 1937.

Nicolini, Ugolino. "Le mura medievali di Perugia." In *Storia e arte in Umbria nell'età comunale*, 2:695–769. Perugia: Facoltà di lettere e filosofia dell'Università, 1971.

Nilakanta Sastri, K. A. *Studies in Cola History and Administration*. Madras: University of Madras, 1932.

Novísima Recopilacion de las leyes de España. 6 vols. Madrid, 1805–29.

Oakley, Francis. *The Political Thought of Pierre d'Ailly*. New Haven: Yale University Press, 1964.

Oppenheim, M. "The Royal Dockyards." In *Victoria History of Kent*, edited by William Page, 2:336–88. London: St. Catherine Press, 1902.

Orderic Vitalis. *Historia Ecclesiastica*. Edited by M. Chibnall. 6 vols. Oxford: Clarendon Press, 1969–80.

Ordonnances des roys de France de la troisième race. Edited by E. de Laurière et al. 21 vols. Paris: Imprimerie royale, 1733–1849.

Orlando, Diego, ed. *Un codice di leggi e diplomi Siciliani del medio evo*. Palermo: Fratelli Pedone Laurial, 1857.

Oxford Dictionary of Medieval Latin from British Sources. Oxford: Oxford University Press, 1975.

Oxford Dictionary of National Biography. 61 vols. Oxford: Oxford University Press, 2004.

Oxford English Dictionary. 2nd ed. 20 vols. Oxford: Oxford University Press, 1989.

Pacheco Caballero, Francisco Luis. "La recepción hispánica de la doctrina de la expropiación por causa de utilidad pública (siglos XIII–XIX)." In *L'expropriation*, RSJB 67 (2000): 163–95. Originally published in *Initium* 3 (1998): 383–417.

Pactus Legis Salicae. Edited by K. A. Eckhardt. MGH Legum sectio 1, vol. 4(1). Hanover: Impensis Bibliopolii Hahniani, 1962.

Parker, D. "Sovereignty, Absolutism and the Function of the Law in Seventeenth-Century France." *Past and Present* 122 (1989): 36–74.

Parral y Cristóbal, Luis, ed. *Fueros y observancias . . . del reyno de Aragon.* 3 vols. Zaragossa: Pascal Bueno, 1667.

Paul, Ellen F. *Property Rights and Eminent Domain.* New Brunswick: Transaction Books, 1987.

Paul, Ellen F., et al., eds. *Property Rights.* Cambridge: Cambridge University Press, 1994.

Penner, J. E. "The 'Bundle of Rights' Picture of Property." *UCLA Law Review* 43 (1996): 711–820.

Pennington, Kenneth. *The Prince and the Law.* Berkeley: University of California Press, 1993.

Pennitz, Martin. "Die Enteignungsproblematik in Römischen Recht von der Zeit der Republik bis zu Justinian." In *L'expropriation,* RSJB 66 (1999): 55–114.

Pertile, Antonio. *Storia del diritto italiano.* 2nd ed. 6 vols. Turin: Unione tipografico-editrice, 1892–1903.

Petot, Jean. *Histoire de l'administration des ponts et chaussées, 1599–1815.* Paris: Librairie M. Riviere, 1958.

Pipe Roll 31 Henry I, edited by J. Hunter. London: Record Commission, 1833.

Pipe Roll 20 Henry II. London: Pipe Roll Society, no. 21, 1896.

Planitz, Hans. *Die deutsche Stadt im Mittelalter.* Graz: Böhlau-Verlag, 1954.

———. *Germanische Rechtsgeschichte.* Berlin: Weidmann, 1936.

———. *Grundzüge des deutschen Privatrechts mit einem Quellenbuch.* 2nd ed. Berlin: J. Springer, 1931.

Plummer, Charles, and J. Earle, eds. *Two Saxon Chronicles Parallel.* 2 vols. Oxford: Clarendon Press, 1892–99.

Pollock, F., and F. W. Maitland. *History of English Law before the Time of Edward I.* 2nd ed. 2 vols. Cambridge: Cambridge University Press, 1911.

Pothier, Robert Joseph. *Traité du contrat de vente.* 2 vols. Paris: Deburc Père, 1768.

Prou, M. "Les coutumes de Lorris et leur propagation aux xiie et xiiie siècles." *Revue historique de droit français et étranger,* 3rd ser., 7 (1884): 139–209, 267–320, 441–57, 523–56.

Pufendorf, Samuel. *De Iure Naturae et Gentium Libri Octo*. Facsimile ed., with translation by C. H. and W. A. Oldfather. 2 vols. Oxford: Clarendon Press, 1934. Originally published in 1688.

———. *Elementorum Jurisprudentiae Universalis Libri Duo*. Facsimile ed., with translation by E. H. Zeydel. 2 vols. Oxford: Clarendon Press, 1931. Originally published in 1672.

Quérard, J. M. *La France littéraire*. 12 vols. Paris: Firmin Didot, 1827–64.

"Querimoniae Normannorum." In *Recueil des historiens des Gaules et de la France*, 24:1–73. Paris: Palmé, 1869–1904.

Rahtz, Philip. "The Archaeology of West Mercian Towns." In *Mercian Studies*, edited by Ann Dornier, 107–29. Leicester: Leicester University Press, 1977.

Ramírez Vaquero, E., ed. *Fuero de Plasencia*. 2 vols. Merida: Editora Regional de Extremadura, 1987–90.

Rastell, William. *Collection in English of the Statutes . . . Now in Force*. London: Thomas Wight and Bonham Norton, 1598.

Recopilacion de las leyes destos reynos, hachas por mandato de la majestad catolica del rey don Felipe Segundo. 3 vols. Madrid: C. de Barrio y Angulo & D. Diaz de la Carrera, 1640–41.

Reddaway, T. F. *The Rebuilding of London after the Great Fire*. London: Jonathan Cape, 1940.

Reeve, Andrew. *Property*. London: Macmillan, 1986.

Reid, John P. *Constitutional History of the American Revolution: The Authority of Rights*. Madison: University of Wisconsin Press, 1986.

——— *Constitutional History of the American Revolution: The Authority to Tax*. Madison: University of Wisconsin Press, 1987.

Reuter, Timothy. "Assembly Politics in Western Europe from the Eighth Century to the Twelfth." In *The Medieval World*, edited by Peter Linehan and J. L. Nelson, 432–50. London: Routledge, 2001.

Reynolds, Susan. "Did All the Land Belong to the King?" In *In Laudem Ierosolymitani: Studies in Crusades and Medieval Culture in Honour of Benjamin Z. Kedar*, edited by I. Shagrit et al., 263–71. Aldershot: Ashgate, 2007.

———. "The Emergence of Professional Law in the Long Twelfth Century." *Law and History Review* 21 (2003): 347–66.

———. *Fiefs and Vassals: The Medieval Evidence Reinterpreted*. Oxford: Clarendon Press, 1994.

———. "The History of the Idea of Incorporation or Legal Personality: A Case of Fallacious Teleology." In Reynolds, *Ideas and Solidarities of the Medieval Laity*.

———. "The Idea of the Nation as a Political Community." In *Power and the Nation*, edited by L. Scales and O. Zimmer, 54–66. Cambridge: Cambridge University Press, 2005.

———. *Ideas and Solidarities of the Medieval Laity*. Aldershot: Ashgate, 1995.

———. *Kingdoms and Communities in Western Europe, 900–1300*. 2nd. ed. Oxford: Clarendon Press, 1997.

———. "Medieval *Origines Gentium* and the Community of the Realm." *History* 68 (1983): 375–90. Reprinted in Reynolds, *Ideas and Solidarities of the Medieval Laity*.

———. "Secular Power and Authority in the Middle Ages." In *Power and Identity: Essays in Memory of Rees Davies*, edited by H. Pryce and J. Watts. Oxford: Oxford University Press, 2007.

Richard, Alfred. *Histoire des comtes de Poitou*. Paris: A. Picard, 1903.

Richard, Fitz Nigel. *Dialogus de Scaccario*. Edited by Charles Johnson. London: Nelson, 1950.

Richthoven, Karl von, ed. *Friesische Rechtsquellen*. Berlin: Nicolaische Buchhandlung, 1840.

Rigg, J. M., ed. *Select Pleas, Starrs and Other Records of the Exchequer of the Jews*. Selden Society, vol. 15. London: Selden Society, 1902.

Riley, Patrick. "Social Contract Theory and Its Critics." In *Cambridge History of Eighteenth-Century Political Thought*, edited by M. Goldie and R. Wokler, 347–75. Cambridge: Cambridge University Press, 2006.

Roberts, J. M., and J. Hardman, eds. *French Revolution Documents*. 2 vols. Oxford: Blackwell, 1966–72.

Rohland, Woldemar von. *Zur Theorie und Praxis der deutschen Enteignungsrecht*. Leipzig: E. Bidder, 1875.

Roman, M. "Les statuts accordés à la ville d'Embrun par l'archevêque et le dauphin après la révolte de 1253." *Bulletin historique et philologique du comité des travaux historiques* (1888): 45–64.

Roncini, Amadio, ed. *Statuta communis Parmae*. 4 vols. Parma: Ex Officina Petri Fiaccadorii, 1855.

Rosenthal, Jean-Laurent. *The Fruits of Revolution: Property Rights, Litigation, and French Agriculture, 1700–1860*. Cambridge: Cambridge University Press, 1992.

Rotuli Chartarum. Edited by T. D. Hardy. London: Record Commission, 1887.

Rotuli Litterarum Clausarum. Edited by T. D. Hardy. 2 vols. London: Record Commission/Public Record Office, 1833–44.

Rotuli Parliamentorum. 6 vols. London: Record Commission, 1767–77.

Roussseau, Jean-Jacques. *Oeuvres complètes*. Edited by B. Gagnebin and M. Raymond. 5 vols. Paris: Gallimard, 1959–95.

Rowley, Trevor, ed. *The Origins of Open Field Agriculture*. London: Croom Helm, 1981.

Rudolph, F., ed. *Kurtrierische Städte*. Vol. 1: *Trier*. Bonn: P. Hanstein, 1915.

Ryan, Alan. *Property*. Milton Keynes: Open University Press, 1987.

Rymer, T., ed. *Foedera*. 2nd ed. 3 vols. in 6. London: Record Commission, 1816–30.

Sackman, James, et al., eds. *Nichols' The Law of Eminent Domain*. Revised 3rd ed. 12 vols. New York: Matthew Bender, 1973.

Salvioli, Giuseppe. *Trattato di storia del diritto italiano*. 6th ed. Turin: Unione Tipografico-Editrice Torinese, 1908.

Samhaber, Konrad. *Das k. bayerische Gesetz des Grundeigenthums für offentliche Zwecke vom 17ten November 1837*. Würzburg: Stahel'sche Buchhandlung, 1839.

Scales, Len. "Late Medieval Germany: An Under-Stated Nation?" In *Power and the Nation*, edited by L. Scales and O. Zimmer, 166–91. Cambridge: Cambridge University Press, 2005.

Schapera, Isaac. *Native Land Tenure in the Bechuanaland Protectorate*. Lovedale: Lovedale Press, 1943.

Schiaparelli, L., ed. *Diplomi di Berengario I*. FSI no. 35. Rome: Istituto Storico Italiano, 1903.

———, ed. *Diplomi di Ugo e di Lotario*. FSI no. 38. Rome: Istituto Storico Italiano, 1924.

Schöffer, I. "The Batavian Myth during the Sixteenth and Seventeenth Centuries." In *Some Political Mythologies*, edited by J. S. Bromley and E. H. Kossmann, 78–101, The Hague: Nijhoff, 1975.

Schulz, Fritz. *Classical Roman Law*. Oxford: Clarendon Press, 1951.

———. *Principles of Roman Law*. 2nd ed. Oxford: Clarendon Press, 1956.

Scott, James C. *Domination and the Arts of Resistance*. New Haven: Yale University Press, 1990.

Scott, Jonathan. *England's Troubles: Seventeenth-Century English Political*

Instability in European Context. Cambridge: Cambridge University Press, 2000.
Scott, William B. *In Pursuit of Happiness: American Conceptions of Property from the Seventeenth to the Twentieth Century*. Bloomington: Indiana University Press, 1977.
Sechi, Antonietta. *La Certosa di Trisulti da Innocenzo III al'concilio di Costanza*. Salzburg: Universität Salzburg Institut fur Anglistik und Amerikanistik, 1981.
Sée, Henri. *Les idées politiques en France au xviie siècle*. Paris: Marcel Giard, 1923.
Sheddick, Vernon. *Land Tenure in Basutoland*. London: Commonwealth Relations Office, 1954.
Shurtleff, B., ed. *Records of the Colony of New Plymouth*. 12 vols. Boston: W. White, 1855–61.
Sidney, Algernon. *Discourses concerning Government*. 2 vols. Edinburgh: G. Hamilton and J. Balfour, 1750.
Sieyès, Emmanuel-Joseph. *Qu'est-ce que le Tiers-Etat?* Edited by E. Champion. Paris: Société de l'histoire de la révolution française, 1888.
Silvestrelli, Maria Rita. "L'edilizia pubblica del commune di Perugia: Dal 'Palatium comunis' al 'Palatium novum populi.'" In *Società e istituzioni dell'Italia comunale: L'esempio di Perugia*, 1:482–604. Perugia: Deputazione di Storia Patria per l'Umbria, 1958.
Simmonds, Jack, and G. Biddle. *The Oxford Companion to British Railway History*. Oxford: Oxford University Press, 1997.
Sommerville, Johann P. *Royalists and Patriots: Politics and Ideology in England, 1603–1640*. London: Longman, 1999.
Stair, James Dalrymple, Viscount. *Institutions of the Law of Scotland*. Edited by D. M. Walker. Edinburgh: Edinburgh University Press, 1981. Originally published in 1681.
Statutes at Large. 18 vols., London: Charles Eyre, 1723–1821.
Statutes of the Realm. Edited by A. Luders et al. London: Record Commission, 1810–28.
Stoebuck, W. B. "A General Theory of Eminent Domain." *Washington Law Review* 47 (1972): 553–608.
Stolleis, Michael. *Geschichte des öffentlichen Rechts in Deutschland*. 3 vols. Munich: Beck, 1988–99.
Struve, Tilman. "The Importance of the Organism in the Political Theory

of John of Salisbury." In *The World of John of Salisbury*, edited by M. Wilks, 303–17. Oxford: Blackwell, 1984.

Suárez, Francisco. *Selections from Three Works*. Edited by J. Brown Scott et al. 2 vols. Oxford: Clarendon Press, 1944.

Taggart, Michael. "Expropriation, Public Purpose and the Constitution." In *The Golden Metwand and the Crooked Cord: Essays in Public Law in Honour of Sir William Wade QC*, edited by C. Forsyth and I. Hare, 91–112. Oxford: Clarendon Press, 1998.

Taglienti, Atanasio. *Il monastero di Trisulti e il castello di Collepardo: Storia e documenti*. Rome: Strenna Cisciara, 1985.

Tessier, G., et al., eds. *Recueil des actes de Charles le Chauve*. 3 vols. Paris: Imprimerie nationale, 1943–55.

Teulet, A., et al., eds. *Layettes du trésor des chartes*. Paris: H. Plon, 1863–1909.

Thomason Tracts, no. 370 (12): *Regall Tyrannie Discovered*; no. 378 (13): *Out-Cryes of the Oppressed Commons*. (British Library photocopy)

Thompson, Edward P. *Customs in Common*. London: Penguin Books, 1993.

———. *The Making of the English Working Class*. Harmondsworth: Penguin Books, 1968.

Tierney, Brian. *The Idea of Natural Rights: Studies on Natural Rights, Natural Law and Church Law, 1150–1625*. Atlanta: Scholars Press, 1997.

———. "Vitoria and Suarez on *Ius Gentium*, Natural Law, and Custom." In *The Nature of Customary Law*, edited by A. Perreau-Saussine and J. B. Murphy, 101–24. Cambridge: Cambridge University Press, 2007.

Timbal, Pierre-Clement. "De la communauté médiévale." *RSJB* 43 (1984): 337–48.

Tott, François, baron de. *Mémoires du baron de Tott sur les Turcs et les Tartares*. 2 vols. Amsterdam, 1785.

Trabut-Cussac, J.-P. "La fondation de Sauveterre-de-Guyenne." *Revue historique de Bordeaux et du département de la Gironde*, 2nd ser., 2 (1953): 181–217.

Treanor, William M. "The Original Understanding of the Takings Clause and the Political Process." *Columbia Law Review* 95 (1995): 782–887.

———. "The Origins and Original Significance of the Just Compensation Clause of the Fifth Amendment." *Yale Law Journal* 94 (1985): 694–716.

Tuck, Richard. *Hobbes*. Oxford: Oxford University Press, 1989.

Ullmann, Walter. "The Mediaeval Theory of Legal and Illegal Organization." *Law Quarterly Review* 62 (1946): 285–91.

Ureña y Smenjaud, Rafael de, ed. *Fuero de Cuenca*. Cuenca: Urgoiti, 2003.

Urkunden Lothars I und Lothars II. Edited by T. Schieffer. MGH Diplomata Karolinorum 3: Berlin: Weidmann, 1966.

Van den Bergh, L. P. C., ed. *Oorkondenboek van Holland en Zeeland.* 3 vols. Amsterdam: Koninklijke Akademie van Wetenschappen, 1866–1901.

Vattel, Emerich de. *Le droit des gens ou principes de la loi naturelle.* Facsimile ed., with English translation by C. G. Fenwick. 2 vols. Washington: Carnegie Institution of Washington, 1916. Originally published in 1785.

Vazquez de Menchaca, Fernando. *Controversiarum illustrium . . . libri tres.* 3 vols. Frankfurt: S. Feyerabend/G. Corvinus, 1572.

Verriest, L. "La fameuse charte-loi de Prisches." *Revue belge de philologie et d'histoire* 2 (1923): 329–49.

Victoria History of the Counties of England: History of Hampshire. Edited by William Doubleday et al. 6 vols. London: Constable, 1900–14.

Vignon, E. J. M. *Études historiques sur l'administration des voies publiques en France aux dix-septième et dix-huitième siècles.* 3 vols. Paris: Dunod, 1862.

Vitoria [Victoria], Francisco de. *Comentarios a la Secunda Secundae de Santo Tomas.* Edited by V. Beltrán de Heredia. 5 vols. Salamanca: Apartado 17, 1932–35.

———. *De Indis et de Iure Belli Relectiones.* Edited by E. Nys. 2 vols. Washington: Carnegie Institution, 1917.

Waelkens, Laurent. "L'expropriation dans le *ius commune* mediéval." In *L'expropriation,* RSJB 66 (1999): 123–32.

Waldron, Jeremy. *The Right to Private Property.* Oxford: Clarendon Press, 1988.

Wallace-Hadrill, John M., ed. *The Fourth Book of the Chronicle of Fredegar: With Its Continuations.* London: Nelson, 1960.

Webb, Sidney, and Beatrice Webb. *English Local Government: Statutory Authorities for Special Purposes.* London: Longmans Green, 1922.

Wegener, W. "Bergrecht." In Erler and Kaufmann, *Handwörterbuch zur deutschen Rechtsgeschichte,* 1:373–78.

Wehlen, Wolfgang. *Geschichtsschreibung und Staatsauffassung in Zeitalter Ludwigs des Frommen.* Lübeck: Matthiesen Verlag, 1970.

Wheaton, Henry. *Reports of Cases Argued and Adjudged in the Supreme Court, 1816–27.* 12 vols. Philadelphia/New York: Matthew Carey/R. Donaldson, 1816–27.

White, Albert B. *Self Government at the King's Command: A Study in the Beginnings of English Democracy.* Minneapolis: University of Minnesota Press, 1933.

Wickham, Chris. *Courts and Conflict in Twelfth-Century Tuscany.* Oxford: Oxford University Press, 2003.

———. *Land and Power: Studies in Italian and European Social History, 400–1200.* London: British School at Rome, 1994.

Widukind. *Rerum Gestarum Saxonicarum Libri Tres.* Edited by P. Hirsch. MGH Scriptores Rerum Germanicarum 60. Hanover: Hahnsche Buchhandlung, 1935.

Wiegand, Wilhelm, ed. *Urkundenbuch der Stadt Strassburg.* 4 vols. Strassburg: Karl J. Trübner, 1879–98.

William of Malmesbury. *Gesta Regum Anglorum.* Edited by R. B. Mynors et al. 2 vols. Oxford: Clarendon Press, 1999.

Williams, Joshua. *Principles of the Law of Real Property.* London: S. Sweet, 1845.

Woolf, Cecil N. S. *Bartolus of Sassoferrato: His Position in the History of Medieval Political Theory.* Cambridge: Cambridge University Press, 1913.

Zdekauer, Lodovico, ed. *Constituto del comune di Siena dell'anno 1262.* Milan: A. Forni, 1983. Originally published in 1897.

Zurita, Jeronimo. *Anales de la corona de Aragon.* Edited by A. Canellos Lopez. 9 vols. Zaragossa: Institución Fernando el Católico, 1978–98.

Index

Adams, John, 105
Africa, 13–14
Ahab (king of Israel), 10
Albergum, 7, 128
Albert of Bavaria (count of Holland), 68
Alfonso VI (king of Castile and León), 18–19
Alfonso VII (king of Castile and León), 72–73
Alfonso X (king of Castile and León), 74
America, 1, 8, 12, 13, 14, 35, 71; and American Indians, 77–78, 105; English colonies in, 34, 71, 77–84, 98, 100, 104–8, 132–34, 137–38; Spanish colonies in, 93. *See also* Declaration of Independence; United States
Amiens (Somme), 62
Amsterdam, 68
Angers: church of Saint-Laud in, 55
Anjou, customs of, 57
Aragon, 74–75; kings of, 75
Araunah the Jebusite, 10
Aristotle, 114, 123, 127
Arthur (duke of Brittany), 89
Athens, 15, 113
Austen, Jane, 134
Austria, 33–34, 65, 69; duke of, 69
Azo, 89

Baldus de Ubaldis, 90
Bankton, Andrew McDouall (lord), 104
Barcelona, 75; county, 27
Bartolus of Sassoferrato, 87, 88, 89, 91, 121
Bastides, 56
Batavians, 135
Battersea (Surrey), 24
Bavaria, 68, 71
Beaumanoir, Philippe de Rémi, sire de, 56, 87, 99
Belgium, 65, 67
Bentham, Jeremy, 34 (n. 1>)
Berengar I (king of Italy), 23
Berlin, 71
Bills of rights. *See* Rights
Blackstone, Sir William, 34 (n. 1), 42, 82, 102–4, 105, 106, 108
Bodin, Jean, 98
Bologna, 50–51; Dominican friary in, 51
Boniface, Saint, 20
Bordeaux, 59
Boston, Mass., 81
Bridgnorth Castle (Shropshire), 37
Bridlington Priory (Yorkshire), 39
Bristol, 41
Brittany, 89

Bulgarus de Bulgarinus, 86, 90
Bureaucracy, 33, 60, 117, 118, 129
Burke, Edmund, 135
Burlamaqui, Jean-Jacques, 97–98, 102, 108, 132
Bynkershoek, Cornelius van, 67, 70, 71, 97, 108

Caen (Calvados), 30
Cain (son of Adam), 114
Canals. *See* Watercourses
Canterbury, 23; archbishop of, 23; castle, 23, 36; St. Augustine's abbey in, 23
Cárdena, Francisco de, 72
Carloman (Frankish mayor of the palace), 20
Carolingian kings and emperors, 19–23. *See also* Berengar; Charlemagne; Charles the Bald; Lothar I; Louis the German
Carthusians, 36, 53
Castile, 18–19, 72–76
Castile and León: kings of, 73, 75, 126; queen of, 72. *See also* Alfonso VI; Alfonso VII; Alfonso X
Castles, 19, 23–24, 35–38, 43, 54, 61, 63, 75–76. *See also* Fortifications
Catalonia, 74
Cevallos, Jerónimo de, 88
Charlemagne (emperor), 20
Charles the Bald (king of West Franks, emperor), 25, 27
Charles (count of Anjou, king of Sicily), 56, 57
Charles Martel (Frankish mayor of the palace), 19–20
Charleston, S.C., 108
Charterhouses. *See* Carthusians
Château-Gaillard (Eure), 54
Chichester (Sussex), 43
China, 13
Church property, 18–24, 30, 31–32, 35, 38–40, 42, 49, 51, 53, 54–55, 59, 60, 63, 64, 69, 72–74, 77, 100, 128. *See also* Exchange of land
Cicero, 113
Cistercians, 53
Cities and towns. *See* Fortifications; *Scabini*; Towns and cities; Urban planning
Clermont, count of, 56–57, 87
Cologne, 66 (n. 119)
Common or public good: and public use, 107, 108; use of phrase, 9–10, 22, 27, 40, 45, 47, 50, 57, 59–60, 61, 66, 67, 70, 71, 72, 73, 74, 75, 76, 77, 87–88, 92, 93, 95, 99, 100, 107, 113, 117. *See also* Res publica
Compensation: in America, 78–84; methods of assessment, 20, 21, 36, 37, 39, 43, 44, 45, 46, 47–52, 56, 59, 69, 74–77, 79, 80–81. *See also* Church property; Exchange of land
Connecticut, 81
Contract. *See* Social contract
Corfe Castle (Dorset), 24
Corsica, 136
Cortese, Ennio, 87
Coventry (Staffordshire), 40 (n. 23)
Cuenca (Castile), 74

Dante Alighieri, 115
Dauphiné, 59
David (king of Israel), 10
Declaration of Independence, 106, 133, 136
Diderot, Denis, 99
Domat, Jean, 99
Domesday Book, 23–24, 29, 31, 32, 33, 34, 37
Dominium: division of, 90–93, 95, 96, 97, 98, 109. *See also* Eminent domain
Droxford (Hampshire), 38 (n. 15)
Du Moulin, Charles, 98

Easement or servitude, 6; wayleave, 6, 46, 62, 80

Échevins. See Scabini
Edward I (duke of Gascony, king of England), 37–39, 56, 57, 59
Eleusis (Greece), 15
Embrun (Hautes-Alpes), 59; archbishop of, 59
Eminent domain (*dominium eminens*): use of phrase, 1–2, 60, 82, 87 (n. 4), 91, 94–99, 101, 103, 104, 108, 109, 138. See also *Dominium*; *Imperium*
Emperors, 15, 16, 24, 42, 67, 74, 86–88. See also Carolingian kings and emperors; Frederick I; Henry IV; Justinian
England, 2, 8, 18, 23, 26, 30, 33–46 passim, 65, 78, 79, 80, 100–104, 105, 120, 131–32, 133, 134, 135; chancery of, 45; enclosures in, 44–45, 101; exchequer of, 35–36, 37; kings of, 23, 26, 30, 69; parliament of, 40, 41–46, 65, 69, 103. See also Edward I; Henry I; Henry II; Henry III; John; Law: English; Magna Carta; Mercia, kings of; Richard I; Wessex; William I
Erskine, John, 104
Estates. See Parliaments and estates
Euboea (Greece), 15
Exchange of land, 23–24, 28–29, 36–37, 39, 44–45, 51, 52, 54–55, 56–57. See also Church property
Exeter, bishop of, 24

Fécamp abbey (Seine-Maritime), 37
Feenstra, Robert, 91, 95, 111 (n. 2)
Ferdinand II (king of León), 73
Feudalism, 1, 2–3, 4, 17, 41, 54, 60, 61, 63–64, 85, 89, 90, 91, 100, 101, 102, 103–4, 105, 109–10, 115, 123, 128. See also Law: feudal; *Libri Feudorum*
Finnis, John, 126
Florence, 114
Fodrum, 6
Forests and hunting, 31, 57, 67
Fortifications, 3, 6, 7, 23–29, 30, 38–39,

40–41, 45, 47–48, 51, 52, 55, 56–57, 59, 61–62, 66, 68, 70–71, 74, 76, 80. See also Castles
France, 17–18, 25–26, 33–34, 40, 54–65 passim, 71, 73, 74, 98–100, 120, 124, 135; kings of, 55; revolution, 64, 100, 133–34, 136, 137; royal council, 62, 65, 69. See also Law: French; Louis VII; Louis IX; Louis XI; Louis XIV; Philip II; Philip IV; Philip VI
Frederick I (emperor), 86, 89, 90, 120, 125
Frederick William (elector of Brandenburg), 70–71
Freiburg im Breisgau (Baden-Württemberg), 66 (n. 119)
Friesland, 68

Gascony, 61. See also Edward I
Genoa, 47, 121, 125
Gerardo de Corrigia, 49 (n. 54)
Germany, 8, 12, 26, 33–34, 65–72, 96–98, 124, 134. See also Frederick I; Henry I; Law: German
Gierke, Otto, 65 (n. 117)
Gilbert, Sir Jeffrey (baron of the exchequer), 101
Gistum, 7, 128
Goebel, Julius, 106
Goths (Spanish), 27
Greece, 15, 113
Grotius, Hugo, 2, 3, 12, 63, 70, 85, 88, 91, 92, 94–100, 101, 102, 104, 106, 108–10, 111, 130–34, 135
Guillaume le Breton, 55

Haakonssen, Knud, 95
Harbors, 41, 43, 61
Havant (Hampshire), 38 (n. 15)
Henry I (duke of Saxony, king), 26
Henry II (king of England), 35–36
Henry III (king of England), 37, 120
Henry IV (emperor), 30
Henry of Huntingdon, 31

Hereford, bishop and earl of, 24
Highways. *See* Roads
Hincmar (archbishop of Reims), 21
Hobbes, Thomas, 100, 132
Holland, 68, 69, 135; counts of, 69.
  See also Albert of Bavaria; Law:
  Dutch; William
Hospitalitas, hospitatio, hospitium, 7, 128
Hospitallers (knights), 56, 73
Hugh, Saint (bishop of Lincoln), 35
Hull (Yorkshire), 38
Humber (river), 39
Hunting, 31, 57, 67
Huntingdon Castle, 24 (n. 25)

Imperium: use of word, 61, 97, 109
Incorporation and legal personality,
  119–23, 137
India, 13
Innocent IV (pope), 122
Italy, 8, 12, 18, 20, 23, 25, 27, 30, 33,
  46–54, 74. *See also* Berengar I;
  Lothar I

Jefferson, Thomas, 105, 132, 133, 135–36
Jesuits, 64, 77
Jews, 10, 14, 39, 57, 76
Jezebel (queen of Israel), 10
John (king of England), 36, 89
Justi, J. H. G. von, 98
Justinian (emperor of Rome), 16, 47,
  129

Kashmir, 14
Kiel, 66 (n. 119)
Kingdoms, medieval idea of, 114–16,
  118, 123–24, 127, 135–36. *See also*
  Nations and nationalism; *and individual kingdoms*

Lafayette, M.-J.-P.-Y.-R.-G du Motier,
  marquis de, 133
La Mare, Nicolas de, 99
La Mure (Isère), 59

Land Clauses Consolidation Act, 34
  (n. 1), 46
Languedoc, Canal du, 63
Laon (Aisne), 120
Las Casas, Bartolomé de, 93
Launceston Castle (Cornwall), 24
Law, 30, 119, 124, 129, 131; American,
  77–83, 94, 104–9; canon, 23, 121;
  civil, 1, 110; Dutch, 70, 95, 96; English, 40, 45, 91, 102–5, 120; feudal
  (Law of Fiefs), 64, 89–90, 91, 101,
  104, 129; French, 55, 57, 58–59, 60,
  61, 63, 83, 98–99; German, 65–66,
  67, 68, 71–72, 120; Germanic, 90;
  international, 94, 96, 106, 107–8;
  natural, 2, 82, 94, 96, 97, 98, 101, 102,
  103, 106, 107, 113, 131–32; Roman, 2,
  15–16, 17, 18, 24, 41–42, 47–48, 51,
  54, 55, 67, 70, 73, 74, 75, 86–89, 90,
  102, 104, 129; Scottish, 104; Spanish,
  73, 74, 77. *See also* Incorporation
  and legal personality; Legislation;
  Property rights
Legislation, 9, 11, 17, 27, 34 (n. 1),
  41–44, 46, 48–49, 51, 52, 53–54, 58,
  60, 62, 63–64, 67, 71, 77–79, 81, 101,
  103, 116, 124–26, 127, 128, 133. *See also*
  Law
Leiden (Holland), 68; university in,
  70
Leo IV (pope), 25
León. *See* Castile and León
Les Andelys (Eure), 54, 56
Lewes (Sussex), 29
Lewis, John, 109
Leyser, Wilhelm, 96
Libri Feudorum, 89, 90. *See also* Feudalism; Law
Lincoln, bishop of, 24 (n. 25), 35–36
Llobregat (river), 75
Locke, John, 100–101, 102, 105, 132, 133
Lombardy, 54; kingdom of, 20
London: Great Fire of, 43; Tower of,
  39

Lothar I (emperor): as king of Italy, 25
Lotharingia, duke of, 67
Louis VII (king of France), 55
Louis IX (king of France), 55, 56
Louis XI (king of France), 61–62
Louis XIV (king of France), 64, 98
Louis the German (king of the East Franks), 25
Lucca (Toscana), 30
Lyon, 120

Maastricht (Limburg, Netherlands), 67
Madison, James, 133, 137
Madrid, 76
Magdeburg, archbishop of, 67
Magna Carta, 36, 42, 108, 125
Maillezais (Vendée), abbey of Saint Pierre in, 55
Maine (France), 57
Mair, Lucy, 4
Maitland, F. W., 1–2, 103, 115
Mansionaticum, 7, 128
Marino de Caramanico, 91
Marshall, John (chief justice of U.S. Supreme Court), 77
Marsilius of Padua, 127
Martinus Gosia, 86, 90
Massachusetts, 79, 80, 81
Meaux Abbey (Yorkshire), 38
Melanchthon, Philip, 93
Meon, East (Hampshire), 38
Mercia, kings of, 26
Merovingian kingdom, 22
Merton, Statute of, 34
Mestre, J. L., 63, 73, 83
Mieres, Tomas, 75
Milan, 49
Mills, 48, 49, 51, 57, 62, 74, 81
Mines, 68, 75
Montesquieu, C. de Secondat, baron de, 99
More, Hannah, 134
Mortmain (*amortissement*), 60

Moses, 114

Naboth's vineyard, 10
Nations and nationalism, 114–16, 118, 135–37
Nature: and natural rights, 124, 126, 131–33, 136; state of, 94, 96, 100–101. *See also* Law: natural; Property rights; Social contract
Nelson, Janet, 125
Netherlands, 33–34, 65, 67, 70, 72, 96–97, 135. *See also* Law: Dutch
Nevers, count of, 57
Newcastle-on-Tyne, 37, 40 (n. 23)
New England, 81
New Forest (Hampshire), 31
New York colony, 80
Nichols, P. J. R., 109
Nicolini, Ugo, 9, 46
Nonantola abbey and town (Emilia-Romagna), 27, 29–30, 125
Norfolk, 29
Normandy, dukes of. *See* Richard I; William I
Northampton abbey and castle, 35
Northamptonshire, sheriff of, 35

Orford Castle (Suffolk), 37
Otto Morena, 86
Oxford English Dictionary, 101, 134

Pacheco Caballero, F. L., 72, 73
Padulle (Emilia-Romagna), 51
Paine, Thomas, 134
Palaces, 18, 49, 50, 52, 56, 61
Palermo, 52
Paris, 55, 56
Parliaments and estates, 40, 41–46, 62, 65, 69, 70, 103, 117
Parma (Emilia-Romagna), 48–49
Pavia, 23; bishop of, 23
Pennington, Kenneth, 88, 92
Pennsylvania, 8, 107–8
Pertile, Antonio, 8, 46–47

Perugia (Umbria), 48 (n. 50)
Pevensey (Sussex), 29
Philip II (king of France), 55, 89
Philip II (king of Spain), 75
Philip IV (king of France), 56, 61, 63
Philip VI (king of France), 61
Piacenza (Emilia-Romagna), 48, 49; San Savino abbey in, 49
Pisa, 30, 47–48, 121, 125
Planitz, Hans, 8, 66
Plasencia (Castile), 74
Plato, 113
Poitou, 55
Poland, 136
Polynesia, 13
Popes, 25, 49, 122
Portsmouth, 43
Potier, T. J., 99
Property rights, 4–6, 16, 63, 68, 70, 85, 86–87, 90–93, 94–95, 99–107, 109–10, 126–31, 133–34, 137–39; communal and common, 4–7, 8, 27–28, 44–45, 53, 68, 73, 74, 77, 88, 89, 94, 97, 101, 128. *See also* Church property; Feudalism; Rights
Provence, 63, 83, 99; Estates and Parlement of, 62
Prussia, 70, 71
Public good and public use. *See* Common or public good
Pufendorf, Samuel von, 70, 97, 99, 101, 102, 108
Purveyance, 6, 42
Putney (Surrey), 131

Quo Warranto proceedings, 91, 120

Railways, 2, 3, 45–46, 139
Redcliffe (Somerset), 41
Reggio nell'Emilia (Emilia-Romagna), 49
Res publica, 16, 22, 23, 47, 61, 70, 94 (n. 29), 97. *See also* Common or public good

Reuter, Timothy, 116–17
Richard I (king of England): as count of Poitou, 55–56; as duke of Normandy, 54
Rights: bills of, 11, 82, 133; declarations of, 64, 71, 100, 106–7, 133; use of word and concept, 124–27, 133–34, 135, 136. *See also* United States: constitution
Roads, 3, 6, 9, 39, 43 (n. 32), 45, 47–52, 59, 62, 71, 72, 76, 78–80, 102, 107, 108, 125, 139
Robert (count of Mortain), 24
Rochester (Kent), bishop of, 23–24
Rome: ancient, 15–16, 113; and medieval fortifications, 25; St. Peter's, 25, 49. *See also* Emperors; Law: Roman; Popes
Roncaglia (Emilia-Romagna), 86
Rouen, archbishop of, 54
Rousseau, Jean-Jacques, 99, 108, 135–36
Rye (Sussex), 37

Sahagún abbey (León), 18–19, 72–73
Saint-Benoît-sur-Loire abbey (Loiret), 23
Saint-James-de-Beuvron (Manche), 23
Saint-Rémi-sur-Creuse (Vienne), 55
Sandwich (Kent), 40
Sauveterre-de-Guyenne (Gironde), 56
Savoy, 52, 53
Saxony, 26
Scabini (échevins), 62, 67
Schenectady, N.Y., 80–81
Scotland, 104
Servitude. *See* Easement or servitude
Shaftesbury abbey (Dorset), 24
Shropshire, 29
Sicily, 52, 53; king of, 91. *See also* Charles of Anjou
Sidney, Algernon, 131–32
Siena, 49–50
Siete Partidas, 74, 75

Sieyès, Emmanuel-Joseph, 135–36
Smith, Adam, 104
Social contract, 96, 98, 100, 108–9, 113, 131, 132, 134, 135–36
Société Jean Bodin, Recueils de la, 9
South Carolina, 82, 108
Spain, 12, 18, 27–28, 34, 72–77, 93, 128; enclosures in, 77; mines of, 75. *See also* Aragon; Castile; Castile and León; Law: Spanish; Philip II
Stair, James Dalrymple (viscount), 104
Strasbourg, 65
Suffolk, 29
Summenhart, Konrad, 91
Sussex, 28–29
Swainstone (Isle of Wight), 38

Takings: use of word, 8
Taxation, 6, 7, 103, 105, 106–7, 133
Templars (knights), 56, 66
Teruel (Aragon), 74
Thapar, Romila, 14
Theodosian Code, 15
Thomas Aquinas, Saint, 126–27
Tiber (river), 25
Tikopia, 13
Tott, François, baron de, 14
Tours, Saint Martin's church in, 55
Towns and cities, 25–27, 30–31, 37–41, 43, 47–52, 53–54, 55–56, 58–60, 61–62, 66–68, 69–70, 74, 76, 80, 81, 87–89, 120–21. *See also* Fortifications; *Scabini*; Urban planning
Trazegnies (Hainaut, Belgium), 67
Trier (Rheinland-Pfalz), 66
Trisulti charterhouse (Lazio), 53
Troy, 114
Turin, 53

Ulpian (Roman jurist), 24
United States, 138; constitution, 11, 82, 106–7, 133, 137, 138
Upnor Castle (Kent), 43

Urban planning, 3, 37–38, 42–43, 47–50, 52, 53–54, 56, 59, 62, 76–77, 83. *See also* Fortifications; Towns and cities
Urraca (queen of Castile and León), 72
Utilitas, utile, 50, 92. *See also* Common or public good
Utrecht, 69; bishop of, 67

Vattel, Emerich de, 82, 97–98, 108
Vercelli (Piemonte), 48
Vienna, 69
Virginia, 79
Vitoria, Francisco de, 91, 93

Wareham Castle (Dorset), 24 (n. 24)
Watercourses (canals, dykes, irrigation, wells, etc.), 3, 6, 27–28, 41, 43, 44, 46, 51, 52, 57, 62, 63, 68–69, 74, 83, 139
Wayleave, 6, 46, 62, 80
Weber, Max, 33
Wessex: kings of, 26
Westminster Abbey, 24
White, A. B., 118
William (count of Holland, king of the Romans), 69
William (prince of Orange), 70
William I (king of England), 23–24, 28–29, 30–32
William III (king of England), as stadtholder of Dutch republic, 70
William Fitzosbern, 24
Winchelsea (Sussex): New, 37–38, 39; Old, 37
Winchester, bishop and prior of, 38
Windsor (Berkshire), 24
Witham (Somerset), 36, 37, 41
Wollstonecraft, Mary, 134

Zeeland, 70
Zwolle (Overijssel, Netherlands), 67

www.ingramcontent.com/pod-product-compliance
Lightning Source LLC
Chambersburg PA
CBHW021811220426
43662CB00006B/263